ADVANCE PRAISE FOR
RESULTS THROUGH RELATIONSHIPS

"Not reading this book is leaving money on the table. Joe Takash captivates the reader by assuring that people are not in the way of the business process. They are the most important part of it. What brings *Results Through Relationships* to a breakthrough level are the practical tools that create foundations for acquiring sustainable business even in the most unstable of economies."

**—Todd Lillibridge, Chairman and CEO,
Lillibridge Healthcare**

"*Results through Relationships* is a handy guide of simple, but powerful reminders for anyone looking to improve personal and professional effectiveness."

**—Patrick Lencioni, author of
*The Five Dysfunctions of a Team***

"Joe Takash has combined two of the most important words in business: Results and Relationships. If you are looking for a path that will lead you to faster and more certain success, this book is a must own, must read, and must implement—as fast as you can."

**—Jeffrey Gitomer, author of
*The Little Red Book of Selling***

"*Results Through Relationships* provides the sensitivity and secrets to forging great client and customer rapport. If there's such a thing as 'return on relationships' or ROR, Joe Takash has provided the royal road to pursuing it. And, what do you know, he establishes a great relationship with the reader as this fascinating book demonstrates how to gain profit from the people who are right in front of you every day."

**—Alan Weiss, PhD, author of
*Million Dollar Consulting***

"Joe Takash has provided the people in our company with motivational, management, and leadership insights for the past ten years. The speaking and training that Joe provides is engaging and offers practical advice on building the relationship skills we need to be successful."

—**Peter Davoren, President and CEO, Turner Construction Company**

"*Results Through Relationships* crystallizes how business success is most significantly reflected by your ability to build and cultivate the human capitol. In disarming fashion, Joe Takash humbles and inspires you with behavioral insights which lead to better, faster business outcomes. This is a must read for existing and aspiring leaders continually seeking that next level of success."

—**Tom Leppert, Mayor, City of Dallas**

"Joe Takash comes as close as it gets to creating a practical scientific formula for gaining greater results through interactions with others. This 'proof through action' career guide both eliminates excuses and equips the reader with an arsenal of tools to motivate individual and team performance at a very high level."

—**Michael Viollt, President, Robert Morris College**

RESULTS
THROUGH
RELATIONSHIPS

RESULTS
THROUGH
RELATIONSHIPS

Building Trust, Performance, and Profit through People

Joe Takash

WILEY

John Wiley & Sons, Inc.

Published by John Wiley & Sons, Inc., Hoboken, New Jersey.
Published simultaneously in Canada.

For general information on our other products and services or for
technical support, please contact our Customer Care Department
within the United States at (800) 762-2974, outside the United States
at (317) 572-3993 or fax (317) 572-4002.

Wiley also publishes its books in a variety of electronic formats. Some
content that appears in print may not be available in electronic books.
For more information about Wiley products, visit our web site at
www.wiley.com.

Library of Congress Cataloging-in-Publication Data

Takash, Joe.
    Results through relationships : building trust, performance, and
profit through people / Joe Takash.
        p.   cm.
    ISBN 978-0-470-23826-4 (cloth)
        1. Psychology, Industrial—Handbooks, manuals, etc.
    2. Interpersonal relations—Handbooks, manuals, etc.   I. Title.
HF5548.8.T2842   2008
650.1'3—dc22

                                                        2008016812

Printed in the United States of America.
10 9 8 7 6 5 4 3 2 1

This book is dedicated to the best listeners
I've ever known, my Mom and Dad;
to my amazing wife Sarah, best friend
and soul mate; to our angels on earth,
Willy and Maggie; and our little angel
gone to heaven, Althea Grace.
Thank you all for your love, humor, and
unwavering support. You are the world to me.

CONTENTS

FOREWORD

Imagine that you are 95 years old. You are just getting ready to die. Here comes your last breath! But before you take your last breath, you are given a wonderful gift—a beautiful gift—the ability to go back in time and talk to the person who is reading this foreword—the ability to help you, the person who is reading this foreword—be a better professional. More importantly, to give you the ability to help yourself have a better life.

What advice would the 95-year-old "you" have for the "you" that is reading this foreword?

I have had the opportunity to talk with a couple of friends who have interviewed old people—or dying people—and asked them the question, "What advice would the 'old you' have had for the 'younger you'?"

Three themes consistently come up in the answers from old people—or people facing death:

Be happy *now.*

Build relationships with people.

Follow your dreams.

This very practical and useful book is all about building relationships with people.

I think that the title *Results through Relationships* is very accurate. I believe if you even come close to doing most of the work that is suggested in this book, you will improve relationships and achieve results—your dreams.

You will become a better leader, a better salesperson, or a better team member. Your company's productivity will increase.

I would suggest that none of these good reasons is the primary reason that you should use the material in this book to build relationships.

You should work very hard on building relationships because the 95-year-old you will be proud because you did. And the 95-year-old you will be disappointed if you didn't.

In terms of all of the feedback and performance appraisals that you will receive in life—that appraisal of the "old you" who is facing death is the only one that matters. If that old person thinks that you did the right thing—you did. If that old person thinks you screwed up— you did. You don't have to impress anyone else.

If you think I am wrong, interview any CEO who has retired. I have interviewed many. Ask them one question, "Please tell me what you are proud of?"

All they ever discuss are the people that they helped— their relationships—not how big their office was or how much money they made.

At the end of the day, relationships are everything.

The main reason to use all of the good tips in this book is to become a better human being.

If that isn't reason enough, don't do it.

If you are just trying to manipulate people to get ahead, don't waste your time. Life is too short.

Review this book. It contains a lot of great ideas.

Do what works for you. Don't worry about the rest.

Have better relationships with people and a better life.

Be someone who the 95-year-old you would be proud of.

Send Joe a little thank you note when something he wrote helps you have a better life.

—Marshall Goldsmith

New York Times best selling author of

What Got You Here Won't Get You There

ACKNOWLEDGMENTS

To Michael Viollt for your brilliance, trust, and character, and the boundless personal and professional opportunities you've offered. You've been my George Bailey. Your humility and goodness are a constant inspiration. The success of Robert Morris College is an artful orchestration of genius, and you are the captain of that ship. Be proud of the mark you've made in the lives of many, and thank you for your love and friendship.

To Bruce Wexler for introducing me to John Wiley & Sons—without you, these words would not be written, this book not published.

To the Wiley team of Shannon Vargo, Laurie Harting, Jessica Langan-Peck, Christine Kim, and Kate Lindsay—you are all true professionals who are guiding, supportive, and more importantly, polite, throughout this exciting journey.

To my colleagues at Victory Consulting, including the resident intellect, Calvin Iwema; the savant-minded Matt Baron; the plow horse, Joe Tabers; the fiery, creative, and razor sharp Nicole Nashar Andrews; and the scary-intuitive Tim Hoyle, a "selfless" inspiration to my career and a truly good soul.

To amazing clients like Turner Construction, Lillibridge, Budget Blinds, and J.H. Findorff for the partnership you've provided me and our Victory Consulting team—you are winning organizations with quality people, reflective of your well-deserved success. There are too many names to mention, but please know I am forever grateful to your fine companies.

To all the high school and college students and teachers who provided me the chance to work with them in the advent of my speaking career—you served as the breeding ground for my professional development and constant reminder that nothing is more important than connecting with people on an honest, vulnerable level.

To General Motors, American Express, and Prudential—thank you for the early exposure to speak and consult in the corporate big leagues.

To Alan Weiss, an incredible business mentor who quickly edified me on the "business side" of the speaking business, and allows me to quote him weekly to even the very top of the business food chain. In his words, "The hardest sale you will ever have to make is to yourself," and "I'm constantly amazed at how stupid I was two weeks ago." You are a difference maker on many levels.

To the 26 groomsmen who honored me by standing up in my wedding (without compensation!)—I love you all from near and far. Joey C., you may be in a better place, but I'll always miss getting the wind knocked out of me from your bone-crushing, bear hugs.

Finally, I want to acknowledge all the people out there who have a passion for lifelong learning as well as those of you who remind yourselves to appreciate what you *do* have in life. I hope the concepts and tools in this book fuel your engine to continually elevate to that next level of personal and professional success.

—Joe Takash
May 16, 2007

INTRODUCTION: GET RIGHT TO THE BOTTOM LINE

This book has a single focus on one goal: apply the behaviors that get better business results faster from your working relationships.

It does not matter if you are the wealthy owner of your own company, a sales manager for a radio station in a large market, or an entry-level employee at a midsize bank. The common interest that successful people share is the desire to constantly elevate to the next level of performance that leads to positive outcomes.

But let's agree on one absolute up front. If your paycheck requires communication and interaction with people, you are irrefutably, unequivocally, indisputably, in the relationship business. There is no gray area, and the reason is simple: no relationships, no paycheck.

Our relationships with others, and the management and development of them, are integral to every facet of our lives; not just work-related ones, but friendships, romantic relationships, and connections with family members. These relationships can determine the path of our careers, the successes we achieve, the level of satisfaction we experience, and the amount of support we feel from others. As you read this book, consider all the different types of relationships you have and identify a few significant relationships across the various areas of your life that provide you with great satisfaction and allow you to do the same for others. Use them as a reference point for comparison and contrast. Try to choose the most rewarding and mutually beneficial relationships. Reflect on all the benefits of those relationships: financial rewards, trust through complete honesty, communication without hidden agendas, unconditional loyalty, a sounding board for creative ideas, and so on.

In my studies of human behavior for the last twenty years, a resonating consistency has emerged. Most people have at least one relationship that defines what we think all relationships should be, but too frequently, we struggle with our other relationships, especially those that take place at work. Breaking through with almost everyone you interact with to maximize mutual benefits is a challenge for even the wiliest of veterans. Even if we get along well with our bosses and direct reports, we often have other relationships in the office that aren't as positive or productive. The results you may be seeking could include more business from existing customers, referrals to new clients, more responsibility, a completely different position, or an opportunity to earn more money.

This book provides insights from perspectives you may not have considered. It also offers information you've heard about, but that you may not be executing at the level necessary to build trust, performance, and profit.

For example, your ability to become not just good, but proficient, at remembering people's names is far more than a "nice people skill to have"; it's a tangible tool that gets business results. I know this firsthand. People love to hear their name, they feel respected and valued. When people feel valued, trust is easier to come by, performance is easier to motivate, results are easier to get. Yet so many bright people at high levels are fumbling the ball on the field of business opportunity.

In seminars I conduct, I've surveyed thousands of people by asking one question:

How good are you at remembering people's names? Fantastic? Not so hot? Embarrassingly bad?

Over 95 percent of responses fall under "not so hot" or "embarrassingly bad." Many of these are high-level execs trying to lead masses of people, salespeople who need to expand their customer networking base for increased income, and new employees trying to make an impression with a wide variety of colleagues. Yet, they leave money and business opportunities on the table every day. I call this the "big business contradiction."

There are so many things out of your direct control in business, namely company buyouts, mergers, acquisitions, and the ebb and flow of the stock market. However, getting great with names is one example of a relationship behavior that is well within your control. Chapter 7 discusses why we fail at remembering names, how remembering them improves your confidence and connections in business, and offers simple behaviors for you to apply to dramatically improve your ability to remember names. And names are just one item in a microcosm of relationship tools that yield measurable outcomes.

PUTTING A HARD LINE ON SOFT SKILLS

Pardon the abrasiveness, but those who say business relationships are *soft* or *touchy-feely* are clueless. Relationships and the breakthroughs we make in them open the doors to different worlds that expedite bottom-line results. The context of relationships can be undirected and nebulous, but not in this book. We will cut through the fluff and get to the results-producing actions.

The Dysfunctional Evolution of Leadership

See Mary work.

Mary knows her product.

Mary gets promoted.

Mary manages a team of people.

Mary was an "A student" in college.

Mary works hard, but she does not work smart.

Mary doesn't motivate.

Mary intimidates.

Mary feels pressure

Mary thanks no one for contributing.

Mary blames customers and yells at employees.

See Mary get fired.

Sadly, there are many people like Mary who, contrary to their workplace conduct, have a heart of gold. But no one ever told Mary how to recognize others or offer direct and diplomatic feedback. Like most people, she was probably never taught how to listen deeply or how to confront colleagues in a manner that would result in positive outcomes. She was never schooled in behaviors that build trust and loyalty, how to rebuild relationships, or how to discover the motivations that fuel the performance of others.

It's hard to blame Mary for not being fluid in a language she was never taught to speak.

Why Wasn't "Relationship Management 101" Offered in School?

If I had a dime for every 50-plus-year-old manager who came up to me after a keynote presentation and said, "If they had taught us these skills when we were starting out, I'd be a lot richer and our company would be more successful," I'd sell my prom tux and buy a new one.

It flies in the face of logic that we interact with people in a variety of positions with different objectives and agendas, and yet no instruction manuals were ever created that cover the how-tos of making positive links with people, which is the lifeblood of business relationships and bottom-line results.

Companies are spending millions of dollars on process-based tools like accounting systems, organizational matrixes, and web-based applications. They're necessary for efficiency and business competition, and I applaud those investments. Yet, the investment to help people develop the relationship tools and show them how these behaviors impact the ledger are grossly imbalanced relative to the focus on business process.

BEHAVIORS OR BUST

Three years ago, I spoke to a team of executives who had just come back from the west coast for a week of "Internal Leadership Focus." They were elated because the consultants had "nailed their personalities." The execs bragged about how throughout the testing and evaluations they had endured, each had understood his or her hidden drivers and the reasons they behaved the way they did.

I followed up with a simple inquiry: "That's great. So what specific behaviors are you going to implement to improve relationships and business?" The answer: silence. Not a single leader could talk specifically about a disciplined behavior plan to change outcomes and elevate themselves to new levels of performance!

I'm both a fan and a heckler when it comes to personality assessments. I love what the Disc Personality Test, Forte Communication Profile, Winslow Assessment, and Meyers Briggs test can do for self-awareness and the understanding of others. My firm uses some of these instruments in executive development. However, I loathe the thought of no attached behavioral plan to yield higher results. Don't we make investments to see higher returns?

This is like my wife telling me the first day of our marriage, "Honey, I notice you never make the bed" and me saying, "Huh, I never thought of it before." Then, three years later over a heated discussion she says, "Do you know in all

the time we've been married, you've never made the bed?"
And I respond, "No I haven't, but I'm *aware* of it now."

ACTIONS GET OUTCOMES

If behaviors don't change for the better, then results don't improve.

You'll see this axiom inscribed in a variety of ways
throughout the book. (Repetition breeds retention.)

If you do nothing else but apply these behaviors, you will
increase the probability of getting better business results
faster. I implore you to understand the context, read the
stories, and raise your awareness around the specific steps
that are laid out in the chapters that follow. You will realize
great value with this approach.

But I'm a realistic optimist. People buy 15 song CDs
for three tracks, buy DVDs for two specific scenes, and
read books to meet their own objectives. If all you want to
do is extract the action-based tools for change, you have a
fan base of one right here. Do what works for you.

WARNING: THE HIGHER YOU GO, THE BIGGER
THE BLINDSPOTS

I research statistics in books, surveys, and studies all the
time. My firm has been fortunate to produce some revealing statistical "science" in our client work—even at less
formal, but highly informative levels. For example, 97 percent of unhappy customers don't complain, and for every 1
unhappy customer, 24 others experience some degree of
dissatisfaction. Even worse, those unhappy 24 will each
tell 20 others about your failings as a service provider. The
damage is exponential, and it can happen with internal as
well as external customers.

In speaking to large audiences and facilitating small groups, I've repeatedly learned the higher the professional position, the less honest feedback people receive about their relationship ineffectiveness, and the more their behavior impacts results. This includes even the "natural born leaders" and brilliant intellects with great business minds.

Fact: Everyone has blindspots.

A few years ago, I coached Tom, a senior executive at an industry-leading company. Having worked at this company for over 40 years, Tom possessed more knowledge about the company and the industry than the other 4,000 employees. His expertise was unmatched, and his ideas and information should be helping everyone from neophytes to senior managers do their jobs better.

However, few people took advantage of Tom's knowledge; they complained that he was cold and rude. These complaints were the main reason I was called in to coach Tom. During our first meeting, I, too, was struck by his gruff and defensive tone of voice as well as his abruptness. He frequently was defensive when I asked him questions about why people didn't come to him for help. He rarely smiled and interrupted frequently.

I videotaped this first session and played it back for him later that day. Within a few minutes of watching the tape, I could see it was having a powerful effect on him. A big, tough guy, Tom isn't someone who wears his emotions on his sleeve but, after viewing the tape, he looked like someone who had just viewed a particularly scary horror movie.

"What are you feeling right now?" I asked him when the tape was finished playing.

After almost a minute of silence, he finally said, "For 42 years, the person inside here (he pointed at his chest) was not that person (he pointed at the television monitor). Why didn't I know all this early in my career?"

During our discussions, Tom came to understand that his relationships were purely functional; that his poor listening skills and unwillingness to admit fault or show vulnerability prevented others from considering him a resource. Perhaps even more significant, Tom realized that his own growth and career had been unnecessarily stunted by his poor relationship skills. He had done well in the company, but he could and should have done much better if he had put more effort in forming mutually beneficial relationships. Instead of being perceived as a resource of wisdom and knowledge and a leader who made a difference in many careers, he was seen as arrogant and intimidating, the opposite of what he wanted.

Not every client project has a storybook ending. This one did. Tom wanted to change for the better (a critical component of this book) and he began using the relationship principles you will learn here to encourage others to hold him accountable for results.

Even though Tom was at an age when people are often set in their ways, he was able to make changes in how he related to others, and that not only allowed other employees to benefit from his wisdom but also helped Tom become a much more valued member of the company.

I am confident that the stories, lessons, and techniques covered here will raise your awareness of how you relate to other businesspeople and provide you the tools to change. Most of us labor in blissful ignorance about the true effect we have on others.

SIMPLICITY CREATES SUSTAINABILITY

Each chapter of this book focuses on one key relationship principle: Offer honest and direct feedback, develop an acute sense of listening, get to know the complete person, and so on.

Within each chapter, you'll find exercises, checklists, and other tools to help you put these principles into practice. You'll also find stories taken from my experiences as a consultant and coach of people who have learned how to create relationships that produce great results. Stories are important ways to learn, and they illuminate learning and understanding in ways that simple explanation does not.

HOW PEOPLE BEHAVE AND WHY THEY DON'T CHANGE

As a speaker, consultant, and coach, I have spent over 20 years working on a wide range of issues with my clients, but these issues usually boil down to this section's heading. It doesn't matter whether I'm called on to deal with dysfunctional teams, to coach a talented but flawed leader, to increase profit, or to improve productivity and morale; there is always a relationship issue. There may be other issues contributing to the problem, but relationships always play a large part in the cause of the problem . . . and in its solution.

Having worked with a variety of individuals from CEOs to new hires, at a wide range of organizations, from large companies such as General Motors, Prudential, American Express, and Turner Construction to smaller, entrepreneurial companies, I can assure you that it doesn't make a difference what people's titles are or where they work. Time after time, I see talented, smart individuals who need to change the way they relate to others to be more effective and successful, but they are unwilling to change.

That's why I developed this relationships-for-results approach. I needed a method to help people change and teach them to form the types of partnering relationships where the sum is greater than the whole. Over time, I've developed and refined this method, creating the concepts and tools you'll find here. Unique concepts, such as using the power of feedback to create stronger relationships will be explained. A coach can talk until he's blue in the face trying to convince someone to change negative behaviors, but when that individual receives honest and continuous feedback, he is motivated to do things differently. In our earlier example, Tom went 42 years failing to establish a single partnering relationship, and it was only through the feedback device of our videotaped session that he "saw" the evidence that he needed to change.

The art of soliciting and using feedback will be discussed in detail. To maximize its impact on relationships, you need to know how to request feedback, who to request it from, and how to process what you hear.

Defensive reactions and denial make even the best feedback worthless. Similarly, if people aren't being honest with you, what you hear can be counterproductive. When you obtain the right feedback from the right person and you're open to whatever is said, you can leverage the information and insights in productive ways. It can help you make small but significant changes in how you interact with others, and it can create a bond between you and the feedback giver.

I have witnessed how important strong work relationships are and how they create bonds that generate trust, performance, and profit. As people learn to be honest and open with each other—as they stop being afraid of being vulnerable—trust naturally develops. Similarly, their performance improves because they're not holding back ideas or critiques—they're not afraid to suggest cutting-edge or controversial approaches or tell the other person that he or she may be doing something ineffectively. Invariably, these partnership relationships impact the bottom line because people are able to focus on team and organizational goals rather than be distracted by hidden agendas, personality conflicts, and other factors that diminish contributions to business goals.

I'm going to share the lessons I've learned from my relationship coaching and consulting work, providing you with dos and don'ts that will make it easier for you to establish and maintain results-producing relationships.

HOW THIS BOOK WILL HELP YOU

Senior Manager to CEO

This results-focused guide is also relevant for people in leadership positions. Too often, executives, presidents, and CEOs retain a command-and-control mentality when it comes to their employees. Their ego and power cause them to rely too much on telling others what to do and not listening to what they need. (Although, many believe they listen regardless of what the empirical data from their troops may provide.)

Leaders are much more effective when they establish relationships that are equal in terms of knowledge exchanges, verbal support, listening, and joint accountabilities. While the need for someone to have ultimate power always creates a degree of inequality, relationships can still flourish if partnering exists on other levels without hierarchal authority.

I have included some examples and advice that pertains to people who are in positions of power as well as for those who are managing down. Nonetheless, the more challenging relationships to create and maintain are those where you are managing up, so the majority of my points are specific to these relationships.

Career Starters to Middle Managers

Many of you have enjoyed some success, but you want more. However, it's likely you still experience frustration in both your relationships and career progress or opportunity.

You know you have the talent to do better than you've done, but something has been holding you back. You believe if you could establish better relationships with people in positions of influence—or perhaps it's just one person, a boss, a customer, or a top executive—your career might blossom.

Your reasoning is sound, though the relationship you have envisioned might not be the relationship that should be established. Just currying favor with someone in a position of authority will get you nowhere—at least from the perspective of long-term growth and career achievement. You can play politics and do favors for someone with clout, and you might receive some short-term benefits. Yet, if reciprocal benefits and foundational trust are not established, the relationships you seek with those of perceived influence will not be sustained.

You want deep, long-lasting, and mutual relationships. Form one, and it can make a difference in your performance and your career. Make a number of these relationships, and they will make a huge difference; that's the very purpose of this book.

Much of my advice is about forming relationships with bosses, customers, clients, and other people of influence. You'll see crucial insights and pragmatic behaviors that work for managing up at this point in your career.

Salespeople, Entrepreneurs, and Business Owners

The relationship partnering advice imparted in the following pages is applicable if you are trying to drive business toward your organization as an account representative in any sales business or as an entrepreneur who must rely on people for results. There are common denominators where you can and should attempt to form the same type of open, vulnerable relationships with your customers and clients that you establish with the people inside your organization.

If you use the tools that lead to higher trust, performance, and profit, you'll achieve results through your relationships—better and faster than what you've currently accomplished, regardless of how successful you may already be.

Maybe you're a salesperson who knows your product and your marketplace very well, you have a diligent work ethic, but you need to connect with your customers with a deeper level of trust to yield higher performance numbers.

Even though you're an intelligent executive who manages your direct reports well with strong influence, do you lack confidence in your ability to manage the CEO or provide him or her candid feedback? Perhaps you're a highly motivated small business owner, but you need to diversify your client base for a more balanced business model.

If you have a core belief that people in business are as or more important than the business process, then this book is for you.

THE BENEFITS APPROACH: HELPING YOU OWN YOUR RESULTS

Creating great business relationships is a process of continual trial and error. It takes courage, consistency, and persistence. In other words, you should practice the relationship-building lessons in this book regularly and even a bit obsessively. If you want to run a seven-minute mile, you don't get on the treadmill one time. Repetition leads to mastery. That's how you'll create relationships that produce measurable outcomes. More specifically, here are three recommendations to optimize your results:

1. *Capture knowledge not information.* Establishing results-producing relationships does not take place from one-time data overload. The mind cannot retain what it does not absorb. It happens from building

knowledge. What's the difference? Information is the "what," but it does not provide you context. Knowledge comes from discovering the "what," the "why," and the "how" to change for better outcomes. This approach is what yields a stronger return on investment, but you have to take this active approach. This is a business book for the purpose of business results. I strongly suggest you do this methodically, by highlighting and making notes. If you capture the nuggets most relevant to your goals, then you capture that knowledge. Owning results begins there.

2. *Talk about it.* You'll see very quickly that feedback and dialogue with others is the bridge to going from where you are to a new level of success. It will also serve as an intentionally pervasive theme as we evolve through the chapters. Throughout the book, I'm going to suggest different conversations you should have with businesspeople you want to partner with. It is also helpful to talk about the concepts in this book with friends and family. They know you better than anyone, and they might be able to help you figure out what you're good at when it comes to relationships and where there is room for improvement. Conversations about creating strong business relationships will also stimulate and help you focus on what you need to do to achieve your relationship goals.

3. *Burn these into your mental hard drive.* If I told you to raise your left hand or recite your social security number, you could do both without thinking about it. Why? Repetition. Rehearsing, testing, recognizing mistakes, and trying it over again are the only ways to make these new techniques second nature. You're going to find a number of exercises here,

from simple checklists to a series of action steps. Use them and, with practice you'll see a wonderful unfolding of multiple crossover benefits. For example, you may practice a certain relationship tool in the Managing Up chapter and see how well it works. As a consequence, you build confidence. When your confidence increases, your creativity and motivation improve. Motivated people perform better, and high performers produce better results. You'll see different benefits from different relationships as you make these steps into habits.

Finally, this book is about adjusting practices not values. As stated earlier, everyone has unique business goals and sees the world through a different lens. I've dealt with the most cooperative clients to the harshest cynics, and they all share the same desires, to be:

- Respected
- Appreciated
- Included
- Challenged to use their talents
- Asked to contribute to something larger than themselves

The relationship model in the following chapters incorporates these five universal requirements, making it a naturally appealing model for both you and those with whom you are seeking high-impact business results. With that thought in mind, let's define what being a relationship partner really means.

CHAPTER ONE

Be a Partner, Not an Order Taker

The lessons in this book may require you to make a fundamental change to your perspective on relationships and business hierarchy. Most people spend their working lives following orders, whether from bosses or customers. These may not be military commands—your customers may ask you in the nicest way possible to reduce delivery time—but they still must be obeyed. This is just the way things are, whether you're a junior executive or higher-level manager.

So here's how to change your thinking: Consider the possibility that you can have an equal relationship with your superior. Regardless of whether your superior is the CEO of a *Fortune 500* company, you don't have to perceive yourself as an inferior in that relationship.

Throughout my years of coaching, I've seen hundreds of productive partnerships among people of unequal status. In high tech companies, entrepreneurial CEOs and geeky techies work together like buddies. In more traditional organizations, senior executives and recent MBA grads participate on teams without anyone pulling rank. And I've also seen customers who treat their suppliers with great respect, generosity, and empathy.

But unless the working culture breeds this, which most do not, these partnership relationships don't just happen. You've got to take a chance, put forth the effort, and make them happen. How do you do it? Well, a good first step is figuring out why you accept the role of order taker in the first place.

TAKING SECOND-CLASS-CITIZEN STATUS FOR GRANTED

Do you accept your work relationships as they are, even if they're not the way you want them to be? Probably. Most people do. Reexamine these relationships, especially the ones where inequalities exist. Most of the time, these inequalities stem from your own attitudes and behaviors, almost as much as from organizational structures and traditions.

Don't be intimidated by conventional corporate hierarchies. While they do still exist to some extent, they are outdated and counterproductive. There's always going to be a pecking order, but that order is changing. In corporations around the world, title and seniority are giving way to talent and its impact. If you've got talent and can make an impact, your contribution will be recognized and valued. So don't fall into the trap of acting inferior to others just because you have fewer years under your belt or are making less money.

Even if you're a senior manager or executive, there's a fine line between cowering before the CEO because of his or her organizational authority and providing the highest value possible because you view yourself as an equal. This single distinction can make the difference in your career (but you'll soon see that it starts in your mind).

Easier said than done? Sure. But you can avoid this trap if you know why people end up in order-taker relationships. If you are conscious of the pitfalls, you can sidestep them more easily.

There are four situations that cause people to accept unequal relationships:

1. Class separation
2. Unequal treatment
3. Listening imbalance
4. Erosion of self-worth

Class Separation

In most companies, many factors exist that create a sense of inequality. This inequality can be perpetuated by the use of titles that divide people into two categories: bosses/direct reports, superiors/subordinates, customers/suppliers, executive vice presidents/administrative assistants. Experience is another factor—senior people tend to be deferred to, especially senior people with a long tenure. Education is also a factor—people who graduated from top MBA programs are too often perceived as *better than* those who went to state schools. In some companies, certain functions or teams have more cachet than others. And then there are those who receive the perks that clearly mark them as belonging to the upper class—corner offices, generous expense accounts, coffee with the boss, and so on.

Unequal Treatment

People tend to define their roles based on how they are treated by their bosses or customers. This is a typical example for a newly hired lawyer. John begins his first day as a junior associate at a prestigious law firm, showing up at the appointed 7:30 AM time. Mark, his boss, doesn't arrive until 8:30 AM. Mark greets John who has been sitting in the waiting area outside of his office with, "John, I've got a lot of work to give you. Follow me."

The interaction lasted only a few seconds, but the impact on the relationship between Mark and John was huge:

- *Tone and pace:* Mark's words and tone of voice said that he was all business and made John feel like a lackey about to receive his assignments. The cold, fast nature of the exchange said to John that his role was to obey without question.

- *Bad manners:* Mark didn't apologize for being late. Nor did he welcome John to the law firm. Being rude tells John that he is so far down on the totem pole that he doesn't even merit bare-bones respect.

- *Commands:* Mark asserted his dominance by his choice of words. He might as well have greeted John with, "Hi, you're my inferior. Follow me to my office, which is bigger than any office you'll be in for a long time."

Listening Imbalance

Unequal relationships arise when one person does all the talking and the other person does all the listening. Test this concept by thinking about your relationships. I'd bet in every relationship where you're the primary listener, you're also the primary order taker. Just as our best friends tend to be good listeners, our best work relationships are characterized by two-way listening.

Erosion of Self-Worth

If you encounter characteristics (tone and pace, bad manners, commands) similar to those in the previous exchange between Mark and John, you could begin to question your contribution and feel inferior. If you are being told you're a subordinate, if a boss or customer treats you rudely, and if this individual rarely listens to what you have to say, you may start wondering if you're worthy of equality. It's easy to slip into an inferior role if that's the role you believe you deserve. Keep in mind consultant Alan Weiss's words: "The hardest sale you will ever have to make is to yourself."

I'm going to teach you how to make that sale. It's worth making. Otherwise, you will constantly end up in relationships that keep you going nowhere fast. With that warning in mind, let's look at the opposite side of the coin for the characteristics of results-producing partnerships.

IDEAL PARTNERSHIPS

Before describing what a true partnering relationship looks like, let me reiterate that you don't have to act like a lackey, stooge, or yes-man (yes-woman). Even if that is how your supervisor or manager treats you, you can change the dynamic of that relationship. I understand the skepticism. I had a psychology teacher in college who used to say, "In the ladder of life, we have a tendency to kiss the foot of the person above us and kick the head of the person below."

What I've learned over the years is that you are responsible for and must own the results you get. Let's put more emphasis on that.

You are responsible for and must own the results you get.

If you act meek and mild, that's how others will treat you. While some bosses are egomaniacal jerks, most aren't. In fact, I've known a lot of business leaders with tremendous power who never used it to bully others. Recognize that most of the customers and bosses you'll work with are decent people; you just have to give them the opportunity to treat you as an equal. If you do, they will make a consistent effort to *listen* and talk, to solicit ideas rather than just offering them, to ask for feedback rather than just giving it.

It is true that just because you're capable of having a partner relationship doesn't mean it will automatically happen. You must first be comfortable enough in your own skin to listen, trust, and respect others. I've tried (not always successfully) to adhere to this ideal. A few years back, Tim Hoyle, one of the subcontractors of my firm Victory Consulting, was talking to me about my vision for the company, and he said, "Joe, I'm curious. You've been successful, but sometimes I think you do what you do because it's safe and secure. Are you really happy with what you're doing?"

Tim is an outstanding executive coach with great insight into human behavior. He nailed me with that question, and I suppose my first reaction was to respond defensively. I could have said something like, "Hey, you've crossed the line with that question." But I gave Tim's words serious thought, and the more I thought about them, the more I realized that I had slipped into a comfort zone. Ultimately, his willingness to ask a difficult, potentially threatening question helped me move my company in a more strategically sound and personally rewarding direction.

I had made it clear to Tim from the start of our relationship that I wanted him to speak honestly to me at all times, that the only negative consequences would be if he refused to do so and sugarcoated his comments. Earlier in my career, I'm not sure if I could have handled his honesty. Eventually, I had reached a point where I valued relating to everyone I worked with on a level playing field. Tim and I were relating as partners, not in the legal sense, but as business colleagues and human beings.

Here are the three key traits of partner relationships:

1. *Respect for differences:* Let's say your customer is an entrepreneur who never graduated from college while you're a Harvard MBA (or vice versa). You respect that your customer pulled himself up by his bootstraps, and he respects that you had the smarts to obtain an Ivy League degree. Your differences may provide creative tension but not negative conflict. You may tease each other, but there's respect behind the teasing. Plus, you've got a distinct advantage over a boss and his direct report who share similar backgrounds. You and your customer can look at problems and opportunities from two perspectives rather than one.

2. *Tolerance for faults:* Everyone has flaws and makes mistakes. In successful partnerships, you don't chastise the other person over a lack of knowledge or skill in a given area. You may not like it, but you accept it. Ideally, the person's other strengths or your strengths more than compensate for whatever he or she is lacking. Your tolerance of others also encourages even the most ambitious boss to be tolerant of your flaws. It can be disarming when you accept someone for who he or she is; in doing this, you are also giving your boss or customer a reason to accept you for who you are. More important, fostering tolerance in others also prevents you from hiding your flaws. We've all experienced or witnessed moments when you or someone you know has tried to fake it, fearing repercussions if you were to say, "I don't know." Instead of asking for help, you try to bluff your way through a task. When someone calls your bluff, you're in trouble. You come off as dishonest. In partnering relationships, tolerance makes bluffing unnecessary, and this candor builds foundational trust.

3. *Honest, diplomatic feedback:* If you've ever had a boss who reprimanded you for making a mistake, you may not believe that any boss is capable of offering kind and constructive criticism. In partnering relationships, tearing apart people isn't acceptable. You counteract that tendency by communicating honestly at all times. Forthright communication delivered with kindness and consideration yields results. How can you learn and grow unless your boss or customer is telling you the truth about your performance? How can you learn and grow if these people tell you the truth but do so with hostility and a desire to hurt? The most productive, results-producing business relationships I've ever had or have coached have involved continuous, honest, and caring dialogue. These relationships make me want to contribute my ideas, not just carry out someone else's ideas. These open exchanges are where innovation comes from. When we know that our partner is providing feedback from a perspective of genuine concern, we are able to thrive and learn.

The most productive, results-producing business relationships I've ever had or have coached have involved continuous, honest, and caring dialogue.

While these three traits are essential to a partnering ideal, I should add that it's unrealistic to expect this ideal to exist every moment in every relationship. We're all human, and even when both people in productive business relationships are attempting to respect differences, tolerate faults, and provide honest, diplomatic feedback; they sometimes slip up. Here's a nonbusiness example that illustrates this point.

My family and I recently had breakfast at a local pancake house, and when the waitress brought us our meal, the pancakes were stringy and falling apart. My wife and I were annoyed; how could they call themselves a pancake house when their signature dish was so bad? As I approached the counter to pay the bill, I fully intended to voice my complaint as I usually do—I figured they might have a new cook or there was a problem with their equipment, and they should know about it. The manager was behind the counter and, before I could say anything, he offered me a wide and genuine smile, his eyes sparkled and he said in his charming Greek accent, "My friend, how was everything for you today?"

"It . . . it was great."

Sometimes, you need to temper your feedback. In some cases, you may not want to hurt the other person's feelings. Other times, you may be too intimidated to say something. It happens in the best of partnerships as well as after the worst of meals. I relate this pancake story so you don't have unrealistic expectations about what partnering involves. There are going to be times when you or your partner fails to exhibit the traits that mark a partnership. Don't expect perfection from yourself or others. What you should expect from yourself is honesty most of the time. If you're honest with yourself and others in most instances, you can hold your tongue under special circumstances to keep from pushing the relationship into order-taker mode.

STARTING OFF ON THE RIGHT FOOT

Whether you need to transition an order-taker relationship to a partnership or create an equal relationship from the start, I want to assure you of one thing: this strategy works. I've used this process myself, and I've helped my clients use it. It's effective because it doesn't just change what you do in business relationships but how you think about them. As you'll discover, both your attitude and actions need to be adjusted to create partnership relationships.

Let's look at the questions you can use with a boss or customer when creating a partnering relationship:

Questions to Ask When Forming Partnering Relationships

- What should I know about working with you?
- What is your leadership/working style?
- How often would you like to meet?
- How do you prefer to communicate—by e-mail, cell phone, or in the office?
- What qualities describe your ideal work partner?

Maybe you're worried that you're going to offend people by asking these questions. Maybe they even strike you as presumptuous. If so, I'm going to let you in on a little secret: Other people want to ask similar questions of you. Your boss would love to know how you communicate best. It would make her a better boss because she would know how to motivate your performance. Your customer would appreciate knowing that you believe it's important to get together in person at least once a week. He would feel a high level of service that could result in additional business.

So it's a fair exchange. Just as important, if you don't ask these questions, you're essentially saying, "I don't expect to be treated as an equal; I'm not important enough to deserve the answers." Or, you may think, "This seems risky. Why don't more people ask these questions?" Because most people don't realize that when it comes to business, they are playing *not to lose*. Life is short and that's why this book is about *playing to win*.

If you make a habit out of asking these questions, then you make a strong statement about who you are. You're telling everyone you work with, "I'm confident enough to ask questions." Don't let fear or skepticism stop you from making this effort. Once you try it, repeat it, and make it a habit, you'll get results.

The answers can also help you define your relationships. If you define the parameters of the relationship early on, you won't be blindsided by order-giver demands. When a customer responds about working style by telling you that he expects 24/7 availability, explain that you have family responsibilities, that you play tennis with your son on Saturday mornings so that's out, that you and your spouse treat yourself to a dinner out every Saturday night. When responding to a potential partner who is acting in a superior manner, it is important to maintain positive communication. Rather than be put off by their demands, suggest alternatives that work for both of you. Right from the start, make sure you both understand what is and what is not acceptable.

Asking questions and providing options shows that you want a comfortable working relationship. Asking these questions also provides a good transition for you to make statements related to each of these questions:

Statements to Make When Forming Partnering Relationships

- Here's what you need to know about me . . .
- My working style is described as . . .
- I like to meet at least once every two weeks because . . .
- Let's meet in person when we have challenges—and leave the facts, figures, and dates for e-mails and phone calls.
- My ideal working partner is someone who . . .

Before asking these questions or making these statements, you need to be able to read the other person and anticipate how this process will make them feel. If you have an old-school boss, he may not like your assertiveness. But people are remarkably respectful of those who ask questions and clarify their own preferences.

Framing the questions and statements so that your intention is clear is essential to the success of this process. If you fire five questions at your new boss within seconds of being introduced to her, she may smile at you but think to herself, "This character is highly unstable." If you issue your statements like demands, a customer will soon cease to be a customer. Imagine how you would respond if someone who worked for you walked into your office and said: "Look, here are the guidelines of working with me because *I only work as a partner*. Now, take notes because I talk fast and never repeat myself. I said grab your pen!"

The key is communicating these questions and statements naturally and nicely. In other words, use *kindfidence*.

KINDFIDENCE

Kindfidence is like an herbal tea; it's a gentle blend of kindness, confidence, compassion, and humility. Most people err on the side of kindness or confidence; they ask the questions in a way that comes across as overly soft (uncertain, meek) or overly hard (arrogant, presumptuous). The trick is blending the two extremes, finding a way to be assertive but also polite and respectful. If you can hit the right note, you're likely to receive a kindfident response in return.

Be consciously aware of situations where you can integrate kindfident questions and statements into conversations. It is easier to introduce them when an opportunity arises, rather than forcing a boss or customer to revisit them out of context. Sue, for instance, was a young management consultant with a well-known firm who was assigned to work with an up-and-coming entrepreneur. A recent profile in a local publication noted this entrepreneur's propensity for calling people at all hours of the day or night. This was completely unacceptable to Sue who was a single parent to three-year-old twins. She waited until her second meeting with him—a lunch—where they went over an initial list of ideas for structuring a new venture that the entrepreneur was contemplating. He responded enthusiastically to the ideas, and so Sue brought up the article and some of the positive observations of the reporter. Then she brought up the calls and asked if was a style he employed with his professional service providers. He asked her if that was a problem, and she said it was because of her two small children. Sue offered, "But let me suggest a few alternatives that might help us deal with late night or weekend emergencies . . ." The alternatives proved acceptable. More than that, the entrepreneur received the message that Sue expected to be treated with respect and consideration and that she would treat him the same way. There was nothing wishy-washy about Sue's approach. There was also nothing resentful. She used her kindfidence to deal with a touchy situation, and she deserved the results she earned.

TRANSITIONING RELATIONSHIPS

At this point, you may be thinking that there's nothing you can do to change the relationship with a stubborn command-and-control boss. Not once in five years has he ever asked your opinion about an important issue. Not once in eight years has she ever tried to adjust her style to facilitate your working relationship.

As impossible as it seems, with effort, these relationships can change. Many command-and-control bosses can be dictators on the surface, but they can be decent people underneath. It's not always easy to create an equal relationship with that hidden, decent person, and it can take time. But trying to do so is better than doing nothing. You cannot change people, but you can influence them. Too many professionals jeopardize their professional accomplishments and personal happiness by not trying. As hockey legend Wayne Gretzky once said, "It is a scientific fact that you will miss one hundred percent of the shots you never take."

To help you take your shots and begin to change the dynamics of these trying relationships, here's a three-phase process called "Managing Up":

Phase I—Preparation

- *Set a time to meet.* Don't ambush your boss or customer. If your intention to change the relationship catches her by complete surprise, she may react defensively and not really listen to what you have to say. Therefore, put it on the calendar. When she asks what the purpose of the meeting is, explain that it's about the relationship but don't go into detail. Find a time that's good for both of you, where neither one of you will be distracted or rushing through the meeting to get to something else. Especially with busy executives or CEOs, getting both of you to focus on the relationship and its outcomes is pivotal.

- *Go into the meeting with a plan.* You want to tell your boss that you feel like you're just executing his ideas rather than having any ideas of your own and that your contribution is going to be limited if that's all you're doing. Make sure you know what you want to say, and more important, do some scenario planning to prepare for what you might get back in return.

- *Get premeeting feedback.* Get feedback from people you trust who will be brutally honest with you about your intended approach and outcomes. Are you asking too much? Too little? Are you being belligerent? Are you being too meek and mild? If the feedback makes sense, adjust your pitch accordingly. You'll also gain great ideas from third-party suggestions. This particular suggestion requires openness and management of your ego.

Phase II—Delivery

- *Manage your emotions.* This doesn't mean ignoring your feelings or putting on an act—you want to be genuine—but if you're upset or angry, you're likely to derail the purpose of the meeting. The other person will react to how you say things rather than what you say. Keep your voice and body language calm and controlled; project confidence and certainty but not arrogance and accusation.

- *Get to the point.* State the reason for meeting kindfidently right up front and that you'd like to share your perspective and that you want to hear his perspective. A strong statement is attention getting and provides both of you with a clear road map to follow.

- *Be fully engaged in the exchange, not just your agenda.* Perfunctory listening is unacceptable. Think fast and hard about the points the other person is making. Are they valid? Are they based on a mistaken assumption? Do you feel one of his points is fair and another is not? Keep your mind open and your brain concentrating to answer these questions and consider the other person's reasoning.

- *Push back if necessary.* Don't accept dismissive or patronizing responses. If the other person is interrupting, ignoring, or doing anything that suggests you're not getting through, bring it to his attention respectfully and request that he really listen to what you're trying to say.

- *Review and decide on a next step.* Don't leave things hanging. Instead, summarize your exchange, clarify any misunderstandings that emerge from the summary, and agree on next steps that will help you move the relationship toward a more equal basis.

Phase III—Follow-Up

- *Monitor progress.* Make sure agreed-on next steps are carried out, next meetings are attended, and new attitudes and actions characterize the relationship. If you feel the relationship is improving because of specific actions, terrific—share this information. If not, share this information too and explore why the relationship is still stuck in order-taker mode.

- *Put it in writing.* You may want a record of what has been agreed to verbally. If you think the relationship will benefit from written rules to follow and written reminders about what to do (and what not to do), then write it. Documentation helps people commit to change.

These three phases are action steps that, if applied, make the transition to a partnering relationship easier. If you've ever tried to be friends with someone with whom you had a romantic relationship, you know that relationship transitions can be tough. Also, what works with one person in a transition might not work with another. So keep the process fluid. Step number one in phase two—managing your emotions—may be the key for one relationship. In another relationship, the transition key may be diligent follow-up.

REALITY CHECK: IS RESISTANCE COMING FROM THE OTHER PERSON . . . OR FROM YOU?

Be prepared to encounter some resistance. Many people have difficulty *not* being in control and don't want to relinquish even the slightest amount of power. Others don't like being challenged or have been operating within that order-taking relationship so long that they believe it truly provides the best means for getting things done.

A small percentage of these people are never going to change no matter what you do. A larger percentage will resist but may change given time and your persistence.

More important, be aware that the resistance you encounter may be generated by you! Don't automatically assume it's the other guy's fault. I have encountered this stumbling block often in my work.

Resistance often arises from your own insecurities and fears.

> **PARTNERSHIP AXIOMS TO REMEMBER**
>
> ➢ You deserve respect from everyone, regardless of status, experience, or educational background.
> ➢ The customer is *not* always right, if the customer is disrespectful, rude, or unreasonable.
> ➢ Your ideas have high value . . . but you must share them with others.

I've worked with men and women who think of and talk to themselves as if they're hesitant, risk averse, and don't value their own talents. But these same people are shocked when colleagues do not treat them as partners. Self-perception matters in any relationship, but it matters especially when you're managing up. If you go hat in hand to your boss, then he'll treat you like a beggar. Therefore, you must believe you are partnership material.

If the other person still shows resistance to this concept, there are two strategies you can use to help convince him:

1. *Bring the resistance out into the open.* Conscious awareness of resistance is a critical first step. Maybe the other person doesn't even realize she's fighting against treating you as an equal. Maybe it's a status issue—your boss believes all direct reports should be second-class citizens. Arrange a meeting and be very specific in detailing the problem and your proposed solution. Don't be long-winded or deliver a philosophical talk on the need for equality. Short and simple works best. You may find that a concise description of the problem and a smart, proposed solution can melt resistance. But remember, less is more.

2. *Write it down.* Busy people sometimes have good intentions but bad execution. They may agree with the points you raised in your partnership conversation, but then some crisis arises and those points aren't acted on. If you want accountability, a written document helps. Plus, when it's in writing, you can submit it, edit it, and obtain approval. A written statement also gives you leverage. I've seen conversations get derailed because of the first thing out of someone's mouth. You open badly, your boss gets stuck on the first point, and you can never move the conversation forward. When you've got your argument down in writing, it is much less likely to happen.

REWARDS OUTWEIGH THE RISKS

Don't wait for the right time. Don't get bogged down in what-ifs. The sooner you express your interest in being treated like a partner, the sooner it will happen. Ask yourself how many more weeks or days you can stand being given routine chores rather than challenging assignments. Think about how your career will remain dead in the water unless you're offered the chance to show what you can do.

If you're unhappy being an order taker, you've probably told everyone you know about this unhappiness except the one person you should be telling: your boss. I conduct a coaching seminar for middle and senior managers that covers a specific module on managing up and viewing yourself as a partner. Many participants have remarked that they have a disconnect with their bosses and aren't honest with them about their motivations, concerns, or dislikes. As a result, one of the assignments I give them is to level with their bosses about what they believe is wrong in the relationship. When I assign this task to people, they all admit that they've told spouses, friends, and others what they really want to tell their bosses. So they've rehearsed what they need to say, they just haven't said it to the right person. Once they do finally say it, they find that the relationship improves exponentially. There has been a staggeringly high return of positive transitions simply by taking these steps. But preparation and action are what elicit the highest results.

Benefits of Achieving Partnership Status

- *Promotions, raises, and job offers:* People engaged in partnering relationships tend to receive more recognition and promotions. These rewards flow from the partnership dynamic, where partners feel compelled to make information, ideas, other people, and opportunities available to you.

- *An expanded network of successful business people:* In unequal relationships, bosses and clients have little incentive to introduce you to people who can help your career within the organization or outside of it. They fear that if they do so, you'll take another job, and they'll lose your services. In a partnership, people trust each other not to use referrals to job-hop (unless there is an open discussion beforehand about this subject). People who partner in work situations recognize that they can draw on an expanded network to get work done more efficiently and effectively. As a result, they share mutual resources without hesitation.

- *A great breadth and depth of business knowledge:* Knowledge is power in today's workplace. Knowledge management programs exist because companies value information and ideas. Order-taker relationships are characterized by one-sided data dumping. Facts and figures may move back and forth, but the relationship stays safe and does not improve for you or your company. No one challenges the conventional wisdom or offers provocative ideas. On the other hand, partners don't constantly censor their exchanges. If you were to eavesdrop on a dialogue between two equals, you would overhear a rich back-and-forth flow of theories, what-if scenarios, cutting-edge news, and so on.

- *More opportunities for advancement and profit:* Your boss knows that there's going to be an opening in another department within the month. Your customer is aware that a company with whom he does business is looking for a new supplier. In order-taker relationships, these opportunities are hoarded. They are only parceled out on rare occasions and only as part of a deal—"I'll tell you about opportunity x, if you'll do y for me." It's not just job openings and business prospects that are shared in these relationships. Your boss may tell you about a great executive education program that a local university is offering and suggest that it could help you fill out your resume and make you a more attractive job candidate internally. Your customer may let you know about an upcoming trade conference and recommend a conference seminar that he feels will open your eyes to emerging trends in your industry. Give yourself access to these opportunities. Make others will feel sufficiently comfortable in the relationship that they will want to tell you about them.

- *A highly effective, two-person team:* Order-taker relationships can get things done. Partner relationships can get things done well. Think about how difficult it is for you and your boss to execute a plan or how it seems to take forever before you and your client can agree on a new program or project. Because of suspicion, laziness, or the lack of vested interest, order-taking teams proceed without much energy or creativity. In contrast, partners are much more focused and committed to achieving their goals.

- *Courage:* People who are uncertain and fearful do not maximize their potential and sadly limit their achievements. This not only has an impact on professional accomplishments but on personal fulfillment as well. When you manage up, you draw strength from the relationship. When someone in a position of power treats you as an equal, then you act like an equal. You make more assertive, confident, and accurate decisions. When your boss or customer becomes your ally, you're going to feel more powerful and in control. Someone has your back, so you can take chances you might never have taken before.

Courage means you speak out when you feel someone is making a major blunder. It also means you are eager to offer fresh thinking even though you're aware that such thinking may offend traditionalists in the organization. And it means you're seen as someone who has the courage of his or her convictions. You are viewed as a leader, not a follower.

Pursue partnerships with people of influence, whether they're in your company or outside of it. Remember that this first step in the relationships-for-results process is ongoing. It is the first step, but it is also the goal. All the other steps we're going to discuss will facilitate forming and maintaining partnerships, including making yourself vulnerable, the subject of the next chapter.

IMPACT: WHAT PARTNERSHIP MEANS TO YOU

The question everyone asks me after a presentation is, "Joe, what you said sounds great, but what does all this mean for my job and my career?" It's a good question. Who doesn't want bottom-line results? I hope I've communicated the job and career benefits of partnering throughout the chapter, but I've distilled the impact to its essence, as follows:

- *Trust:* Working within an open and honest relationship, you'll feel free to express your ideas and take on new challenges. It's energizing to work in a setting where hidden agendas are absent and you can be genuine.

- *Performance:* You're empowered to work with greater creativity, freedom from fear (of making mistakes), and the ability to pursue opportunities. As a partner, you take pride of ownership in the work you do and have a vested interest in achieving objectives.

- *Profit:* Your dynamic exchange of knowledge, skills, and feedback turns you into a results-producing machine. You now possess the resources necessary to make more money for yourself and your company.

CHAPTER TWO

Reveal Your Flaws without Fear

Admit it. There are times when you're reluctant to say to a business colleague, "I don't know," or "I'm not good at x." You're convinced she'll be disappointed in you. Or at the very least, she'll decide you're not as capable as she assumed you were.

This is a very human reaction, even more so in business relationships than in personal ones. But it's not the way you should act if you want the highest possible results. There's paranoia in the work place that surrounds accepting blame or admitting that you're not sure how to achieve a goal. It goes back to the idea of not showing weakness to an enemy. In today's organizations, however, your bosses and customers are not your enemies (unless you treat them that way).

Revealing flaws without fear communicates authenticity, attracts others, and is a firm seed-planting behavior that builds trust. The most genuine people in the room are the ones who are the most transparent. They are not hesitant to express their doubts and uncertainties as well as their visions and values. People love to work with individuals who are authentic. It ratchets relationships up to new levels—levels where people are eager to give as well as receive.

The following story illustrates the challenges that often prevent people from making themselves vulnerable.

TURN A MISSED OPPORTUNITY INTO A MADE ONE

Have you ever committed an incredibly bad business blunder? Have you ever experienced that awful, roller-coaster stomach-dropping moment when you realize that you messed up? It's an uncomfortable feeling, and most of us try to cover up the mistake. We make excuses, offer rationalizations, and do everything but take responsibility for our errors.

I was invited to be a speaker at a client's national sales conference in Las Vegas. The client, Budget Blinds, was bringing in one of the country's top motivational speakers to deliver the opening keynote, and I was asked to do three breakout sessions. It was a great opportunity, and I was looking forward to the March 3rd event.

Only the event was actually March 2nd. I learned I had the wrong date when I was in Dallas completing a two-day seminar for another client. At noon on the 2nd, I received a voicemail message from Tracy, my Budget Blinds contact: "Joe, this is Tracy, and I'm very worried. I checked the front desk, and they say you haven't checked in, and I have a group of 200 attendees waiting for you to speak."

I take pride in living my word, personally and professionally. As you can imagine, the realization of my mistake triggered a massive panic attack, not to mention some less than professional self-directed language. Embarrassed and aghast, I called Tracy, admitted my scheduling error and promised I would do everything possible to get to the

Las Vegas conference quickly, but I needed to finish my seminar in Dallas. She told me she had to talk to some other people and would call me back. When she called an hour later, she told me she had the five founders of Budget Blinds on the line.

My first thought was to come up with an excuse to make my mistake seem more palatable. I could tell them how busy I had been, how there wasn't much harm done because I could get there tomorrow. But then I realized that making excuses was the wrong thing to do. It would have communicated that I wasn't taking responsibility for my mistake.

So I said, "Gentlemen, I cannot express how sorry I am that I've let you down. I've been excited about speaking at your conference and have worked hard to prepare a great presentation. But I made a huge scheduling error. I will do whatever it takes to get back in your good graces, starting with refunding my entire fee."

Chad Hallock, CEO of Budget Blinds, said, "Joe, we've decided to turn a negative into a positive. We've switched the closing speaker to your sessions and we want you to close the conference tomorrow."

This was a great opportunity. Instead of speaking to 200 people, I would be speaking to 800 in the prestigious closing keynote spot.

When I arrived in Las Vegas the next day, all five top executives greeted me with a smile. No one made cutting remarks about my tardiness or made me feel guilty. Although I apologized more than once, they all responded by telling me not to worry about it.

The closing session was one of the best presentations I had ever made and one of the most educational professional experiences I've encountered. The connection with the audience was immediate and electric. I was asked to return the next year as the conference's closing speaker. (I planned to arrive six weeks early after this scarring experience.)

Looking back, I could have responded differently when I was confronted with my error. I could have gone on and on about my busy schedule or tried to shift the blame. But that would have been wrong and would have compromised the most important attribute in human relations, character. More to the point, it would have destroyed rather than solidified a results-producing relationship.

I can't emphasize enough the benefits of apology and forgiveness in cementing relationships. My willingness to apologize communicated that I was honest and accepted responsibility. Their willingness to forgive—to accept and move beyond my very human mistake—made me want to run through a brick wall for them. This combination of apology and forgiveness didn't simply repair the relationship; it rebuilt it. This is a crucial point.

The best relationships are not built; they are rebuilt.

When two colleagues weather adverse conditions and handle these conditions with compassion and trust, the relationship doesn't just survive—it thrives. Overcoming challenges, setbacks, and even failures in the right way can be an opportunity to take relationships to a new level.

To do so, you're going to have to allow yourself to be vulnerable. This can be difficult for some, depending on previous experiences. This is especially true if you're convinced that if you admit fault, someone will hold it against you or that if you take responsibility for a mistake, your boss will believe that you're careless. At times, everyone has this reflex and reacts defensively to criticism or becomes worried about what others will think if they say, "My mistake." But remember that you are not communicating weakness or incompetence; you're vulnerable like all human beings, and vulnerability is something just about everyone responds to positively.

Perhaps you'll be more willing to embrace vulnerability if you understand the difference between that term and being *soft*.

IT TAKES STRENGTH TO ADMIT VULNERABILITY

People mistakenly believe that they'll never be taken seriously if they admit a weakness or fear or that they'll never make a sale if they acknowledge their uncertainty. No one wants to be considered weak, and rightly so. People who are weak are ineffective, conflict-avoidant, and uninspiring. This is very different from being vulnerable. Table 2.1 highlights the 12 differences between soft and vulnerable traits.

At times, a fine line exists between soft and vulnerable. You may have a soft leader who is everyone's friend, who is a nice guy, who never gets mad and hates when others

Table 2.1 Soft versus Vulnerable Traits

Soft Traits	Vulnerable Traits
1. Doesn't hold self accountable	1. Takes pride in being accountable
2. Avoids tasks outside of expertise	2. Willing to ask others for help
3. Allows other people to slide	3. Assists others in meeting their goals
4. Lets emotion blur objectivity	4. Empathetic but analytical
5. Indecisive	5. Solicits input before deciding
6. Avoids conflict	6. Tries to move others from conflict to consensus
7. Makes excuses	7. Willing to admit fault and apologize
8. Resists change or pressure	8. Enjoys challenges and new learning
9. Wishy-washy	9. Strong beliefs
10. Uninspiring	10. Influential
11. Difficult to read	11. Transparent
12. Lacks self-confidence	12. Humble

become angry at each other. A vulnerable leader may also be an extremely nice individual, but his niceness doesn't get in the way of his ability to make tough decisions or hold others accountable. When you're vulnerable, you may seem soft on the outside, but when necessary you can be tough as nails.

Transparency is a good trait to use as a differentiator because people who are soft are usually afraid to communicate with honesty about themselves and to others. They worry about the repercussions of being straightforward about their beliefs. When you're transparent, it prevents others from thinking you have hidden agendas. When you ask someone to do something, you have no ulterior political motives. What you say is what you mean.

When you communicate transparently, you encourage others to respond in the same manner. This bolsters business relationships in many ways, creating a bond of trust that helps people deal with all sorts of calamities and crises. You'll recall my earlier comment that relationships aren't built, but rebuilt. Transparency greatly assists the rebuilding process.

When I discuss transparency with others, people usually apply a different interpretation. They believe that they can speak their mind without any editing. That *hard* stance can, however, be just as detrimental to a relationship as a soft one. There are bosses and customers who are brutal with their honesty. They tend to say things like, "Jenny, you will never go higher than midlevel management because you simply are not a natural born leader."

Being candid is good; being tactless and rude is bad. Transparency fosters results-producing relationships when you use discretion. Think situationally. If your boss is on edge, it may be unwise to unload on him about your difficulties dealing with a client, at least at that time. What you want to aim for is being as transparent as a given situation and common sense allows you to be. Knowing the right timing with others is the hallmark of smart communication.

Sometimes it's a tough call. In certain instances, you may be risking your job or a relationship with a big account by being transparent. But it's a risk worth taking. When you tell your biggest customer that his operation is in need of restructuring, he may resent your presumption. At the same time, if he values your insights and respects your work, he may believe that what you say is what you believe, that you're taking this risk because you really want to help him improve his operation, and you don't have a hidden agenda. It may create a bond that greatly enhances the relationship and what both of you get out of it. Everyone appreciates straight-talk honesty more than a tap dancing yes-person.

It takes courage to exhibit transparency or any of the traits of vulnerability. This is true whether you're just starting out or, as in the following case, the new CEO of a company.

A few years ago, Peter Davoren was named CEO/ President of Turner Construction Company, one of the country's largest builders (from high-rises to hospitals to stadiums) and a longstanding client of mine. After the announcement, Peter addressed a large gathering of employees. Typically, this is the time when a new CEO gives his visionary, big-boss speech about mission and values, projecting an air of unshakable confidence and optimism.

Using a different approach, Peter opened his talk with the following words:

> I'm very honored to have recently been named the CEO of Turner, and the first thing I must share with you is that I feel completely over my head. But where I quickly gain confidence is by knowing that I am surrounded by people like you to help all of us continue to succeed and grow as a team.

Why would the new head of multibillion-dollar pow-
erhouse company reveal his uncertainty? Wouldn't this
admission shake the confidence of employees?

Not at all. Despite saying that he felt as if he was in over
his head, he paradoxically projected strength and purpose
in his talk. Davoren's tone, his words, his body language,
his humor, all conveyed that he was a strong leader with
ideas and a viable plan for success. Nonetheless, I doubt
anyone in that room forgot that he said he was in over his
head. It made it easier to identify with him as a person, a
peer willing to share the fears that every audience member
possesses. From that initial statement on, the bonding was
stronger and the motivation greater.

Over the years, I've seen some brilliant speakers take
the platform, but I have seen few make the authentic connection with an audience that Peter did. His honesty, his
self-deprecating humor, and his straightforward approach
resonated with employees. As one of them noted after the
speech, "It's like he's one of us." Peter achieved this connection because of his vulnerability.

The best leaders, managers, business owners, and
salespeople are vulnerable. Contrary to what some people
believe, projecting invulnerability is a mistake. Customers
don't trust salespeople who always have quick answers to
their questions, never admit uncertainty about problems,
or never demonstrate their willingness to find the slow
answers. Direct reports aren't motivated by a boss who
is cold and flawless; they can't relate to his icy demeanor.
Think about how unattracted and turned off you are by
people who are unwilling to be enlightened or admit fault.

While showing vulnerability can work wonders, if
all you do is reveal flaws and admit mistakes, you're not
going to create results-producing relationships. It's only
when you allow yourself to be authentic about your fears
combined with equal authenticity about your beliefs and
values that relationships move to a higher level. Projecting

kindfidence is contagious and an important term useful for achieving this combination of strength and vulnerability.

A POTENT MIXTURE

Kindfidence is a combination of kindness and confidence, but its impact means much more than those two words. Think about the term as a blending of two sets of characteristics not usually listed in the same breath. On the one hand, you have kindness, compassion, empathy, and humility. On the other, you have confidence, strength of character, decisiveness, and accountability. The combination of these traits attracts others, gains buy in, and is both influential and persuasive.

Now consider each set of words separately. If you describe someone in business who uses only the kindness set without projecting confidence or conviction you're apt to say, "That individual is a pushover." In business, if you use only the confidence set, others may say you have a reputation for arrogance.

It's only when the two sets of characteristics are combined that the negative attributes of each are eliminated. Blending not only diminishes the negative extremes, it also communicates positive values to other people in the business relationship. People who emulate kindfidence have a way to express their vulnerabilities without fear or hesitation. They aren't fretful or neurotic or weak. They can tell another person, "I don't know if I can do that," without seeming incompetent or insecure. Their tone and manner convey that they are able and willing to learn what they don't know or find someone who can provide what they're missing. They don't doubt themselves. Instead, their honesty reassures others that they're not trying to fake it and endanger a project.

Kindfidence can be used whether you're a CEO like Peter Davoren or just starting out. If you're an entry-level employee, your boss will expect you to be humble and uncertain. Yet you don't have to demonstrate fear or subservience. You can come across as concerned, committed, and resolute, even if you haven't yet mastered all the ins and outs of your job. Too often, people place a premium on knowledge, forgetting that if you can't manage your ego; your boss or your customer won't attach much importance to what you say.

People don't care how much you know until they know how much you care.

The contagion part of the equation means that if you relate with kindfidence, you'll prompt the same response from your relationship partner. Human behavior and the emotions that follow that behavior are contagious. Have you ever yawned at a meeting and noticed someone else yawn seconds later? Or been at a funeral for a loved one when someone put her hand on your shoulder to offer comfort, and you felt like crying? At the other extreme, if someone is talking to you in a cynical or sarcastic manner, you're likely to respond in kind.

The more consistent you are in expressing kindfidence, the more likely you are to receive it in return. To help you appreciate the importance of expressing kindfidence consistently, I've listed two common business scenarios, the typical relationship response and the kindfident alternative.

Scenario One

Your boss criticizes how you presented to a client. She tells you that you talked too quickly and sold too hard, that next time you need to take it slower and be subtler in your pitch, otherwise both you and the organization will lose credibility.

Typical response: You react defensively, claiming that your approach was the correct one but that it doesn't jibe with your boss's style and that's why she didn't like it.

Likely result: Not good for your business relationship.

Kindfident response: Summarize in your own words what your boss is telling you, express appreciation for the suggestion, and ask if there might be some specific behaviors between the softer approach your boss is suggesting and your particular style so you will recognize what a more successful approach looks like.

Likely result: Good for your business relationship.

Scenario Two

A major customer complains about your company's new pricing policy. He says that he is being charged for some extras that were never included in the bill before. He insists that his complaint isn't about the money—which is negligible—but about how he has been a customer of yours for five years and it seems to him that his loyalty is not being reciprocated.

Typical response: You cave in and tell the customer not to worry about the new pricing policy, that he won't have to pay the new charges.

Likely result: Not good for your business relationship.

Kindfident response: Talk about how you understand why he might feel that way about the charges, but that in the new, highly competitive environment, the company can no longer afford not to charge its customers for the additional products or services. Explain the situation so that your customer understands how it puts the company at a competitive disadvantage, and that the company would prefer to charge a little bit for the extras rather than raise prices a lot on its main products and services.

Likely result: Good for your business relationship.

These kindfident responses are just examples of how the average person might respond. You need to find your own, authentic way of combining kindness and confidence. As long as you get both across, the relationship will benefit.

TIPS AND TECHNIQUES: HOW TO REVEAL YOUR FLAWS WITHOUT FEAR

One of the best changes that has taken place in all types of organizations is a movement toward more collaborative cultures. In these cultures, the no-flaws leader is disappearing, being replaced by people who are willing to admit mistakes and accept other people's imperfections. In Jim Collins's bestselling book, *Good to Great* (New York: HarperCollins, 2001), he notes that the three most important words a leader can use is, "I don't know." We are working in an era of so much uncertainty and unpredictability that it's foolish to pretend to possess knowledge you don't have. Similarly, people who are so obsessed about being perfect never take any chances. Success today is based on taking reasonable risks and making smart decisions. Leaders recognize that the road to success is littered with mistakes, and so they encourage people to take chances along the way. It's not that managers like it when people fail or mess up, but they recognize that it's a better alternative than never taking a risk at all.

Michael Viollt, president of Chicago's Robert Morris College since 1996, has created a culture where errors are viewed as inevitable, correctable, and even, necessary for growth. Viollt has increased revenues by more than 3000 percent during his tenure, and his tolerance for error has something to do with the college's success. People who work at the college don't view mistakes as something to cover up, but rather as stepping-stones for improvement where they learn and do it better the next time.

With this environment in mind, here are five ways you can facilitate revealing your flaws and strengthen key relationships:

1. Question yourself honestly.
2. Solicit feedback from more than one source.
3. Act in your professional life as you do in your personal life.
4. Rehearse being authentic and open.
5. Make a commitment to apologize and forgive.

Question Yourself Honestly

You may *think* you're open about your problems and fears, but if you think more critically about this issue, you'll realize that you probably do censor yourself. Most of us do. Maybe you're willing to talk about your anxieties with one trusted colleague, but when it comes to your boss, you're Mr. or Ms. Stoic. Like an athlete engaged in a sport, your reflex is to hide your weaknesses so that your opponent can't take advantage of them. However, in work situations, your boss or customer is not your opponent (or shouldn't be). There aren't winners and losers in every engagement.

Still, this reflex is powerful. To overcome it, engage in self-talk around your vulnerability in various work situations. This means carrying on a reflective dialogue with yourself about what you say, think about, and do when you have a chance to exhibit vulnerability. To start that internal dialogue, pose the following questions to yourself:

- When I talk to people with influence/power, do I try to enhance their perceptions of me or do I say what I really believe?

- When I make a mistake, do I point fingers and make excuses or do I take it on the chin, admit fault, and try to come up with solutions to overcome the mistake?

- When I believe that a person of influence is treating me or others unfairly, do I keep my mouth shut out of fear of the consequences or do I speak my mind diplomatically?

Solicit Feedback from More than One Source

Soliciting and receiving feedback keeps you honest. You can't fool yourself into believing you're completely open when everyone is telling you you're not. Therefore, designate a selective group of colleagues to provide you with feedback. Choose people who you can trust and who you can rely on to be objective. Have them respond to the three previous "when" questions.

Feedback is the breakfast of champions.

—*Ken Blanchard*

In addition, depending on the type of environment you work in, it may be helpful to have someone videotape you. I realize that this can be awkward and that your customer may not want to have a conversation between the two of you taped. But there will be occasions when taping is perfectly acceptable—when you're making a presentation to a client or during a team meeting. With the risk of melodrama, I've found that these tapes can transform professional awareness, behavior, relationships, and results. In working with clients, I've videotaped over 3,000 presentations, and not one person after viewing the tape has said, "I was phenomenal."

As the old saying goes, "The camera doesn't lie." You may discover that you are striking a pose or acting a part rather than being yourself. You may see how you become defensive or rationalize. Whatever the tape shows, it will help make you aware of how you're shielding yourself from others. Many people believe they are showing passion and concern, but the video proof confirms the opposite.

Based on these two types of feedback, search for patterns within your behavior. Recognize that some of the feedback you receive will be contradictory or off point. You can't agonize over every critical comment or negative observation. When you find a pattern of behavior that suggests you react to stress by being obstinate or to criticism by being defensive, then you're on to something useful. Not everyone acts invulnerable in the same way. Some people bluster to hide their flaws while others clam up. Figure out your pattern. By doing so, you'll raise your awareness of it and be better equipped to break the pattern.

Act in Your Professional Life as You Do in Your Personal Life

We all behave differently in different circumstances. However, are you one person with your spouse or friends and another person at the office? Are you much more willing to share your concerns and problems in personal relationships than in professional ones? It is a strange but true phenomenon that we become different, less authentic people in our jobs.

You're going to have to fight against this, and one way of doing so is by being aware if a contrast exists between your personal and professional personas. Think about whether you're friendly, more open, more willing to say you're wrong in one area of your life than another. Ask your friends and family members for feedback, and see if it matches the feedback you solicited from your work colleagues.

While it's understandable and respectable that some people choose to separate personal and professional behaviors, the goal here is merely to close the gap between the two identities for the purpose of more successful business outcomes. Realistically, you may not be able to eliminate this gap entirely; you're closer with your friends and family than you are with a customer or a boss. Yet, if you can move your work self in the direction of who you are at home or at dinner with friends, then you're going to move toward being more vulnerable, more authentic, and more confident. That's what people respond to most in your personal life that directly translates to your professional success—who you are naturally, not who you think you should be.

Rehearse Being Authentic and Open

Plan how and when you're going to be more open and honest. It's great to resolve to change. Better is making a resolution to change and then taking action steps to implement those changes. In the coming days and weeks, perhaps you have a series of meetings and presentations scheduled. Choose specific ones as opportunities to behave in a more vulnerable manner. Write down what you're going to say and do in response to anticipated situations. For instance, you have a meeting scheduled with your boss to discuss a project that you find boring. Instead of acting like you can't wait to get back to a task you find painfully unchallenging, plan on being honest about your feelings. Write an approximation of how you're going to communicate these problems:

> I realize that not all project details are exciting, but is there a chance you could mix in some more challenging assignments with the routine ones? It's not easy for me to express this because I want be a team player, but I simply perform at a higher level when I feel stimulated and challenged in areas where I'm passionate.

You don't have to use the exact words you write, but this rehearsal makes it easier to speak genuinely and without fear of consequences, and it illuminates opportunities for further discussion between you and your boss in the future. It also provides insight about you to your superior that he or she may otherwise never have realized.

Make a Commitment to Apologize and Forgive

Similar to the practice of showing others that you are vulnerable is using the power of apology and forgiveness. Of all the techniques presented here, these two actions may be the most difficult. Saying you're sorry to a customer may feel like you are a criminal confessing guilt to a policeman. Forgiving one of your team members for snapping at a client may seem counterintuitive—when what you'd really like to do is send them packing. But these reactions may be rooted in your own insecurities. Whatever the motive, remember, your most results-producing relationships are not built. They are rebuilt.

Apology and forgiveness will communicate to the influential people in your work life that you value their feelings and judgments. These actions will build relationships in a way that defensiveness and passive-aggressiveness can't.

To help you apologize and forgive, here are some common business situations where you can practice each:

Apology

- ❑ Missed a deadline
- ❑ Took a shortcut to finish an assignment
- ❑ Failed to participate in or contribute much to an important meeting
- ❑ Engaged in time-wasting, unconstructive personality clash with a colleague

❑ Failed to communicate an important piece of information

❑ Tried to fake your way through an assignment where you lacked the right skills or knowledge

❑ Made an offensive remark that was hurtful or unprofessional

Forgiveness

❑ Passed over for a promotion, raise, or salary increase

❑ Given an overwhelming amount of work

❑ Denied the chance to work on an assignment that you've expressed interest in

❑ Not included on a committee or team to which you feel you should have been included

❑ Criticized unfairly (or so it seems to you) or in front of others

❑ Asked to bring in someone else to help you on a project (with the implication you can't handle it on your own)

❑ Treated rudely or coldly when the other person was under stress

BRIDGING THE DISTANCE

Most students of history have read about or recall watching how John F. Kennedy reacted to the Bay of Pigs crisis. As president, he was responsible for bringing us to the brink of a nuclear war with the Soviet Union. Nonetheless, he could have responded politically in its aftermath and justified his actions, diverted attention from his decisions, or named several others as the cause of the crisis.

Instead, he said it was his fault. Even more astonishing than his accepting responsibility was that, after he accepted responsibility for his mistake, his approval ratings in the polls went up.

Contrary to what many people believe, admitting mistakes can evoke a positive response. Now, if someone always makes mistakes, no quantity of "mea culpas" is going to help. Most of us make the occasional error, and taking the blame doesn't stamp us as incompetent.

Far from it. I cite John F. Kennedy here because he was one of the most charismatic individuals to ever hold office in this country. He would not have been nearly as charismatic if he had adopted a flawless pose. JFK came off as a dynamic human being in no small part because he wasn't afraid to admit when he was wrong.

Most business relationships begin with wariness and tentativeness. When they start, people are far apart. They lack familiarity and trust. To create a real partnership requires eliminating a good deal of formality that characterizes these relationships. When you reveal your flaws, confess to your errors, and act in a genuine manner, you can bridge that distance quickly.

You don't have to possess the charisma of JFK to enjoy a results-producing relationship. You do, however, have to act in a genuine manner, and part of being genuine is revealing flaws and admitting mistakes. It all begins with honest self-talk and the willingness to make a smart investment by risking honesty, which has multiple positive returns in terms of trust, performance, and profit.

CHAPTER THREE

Offer Honest and Direct Feedback

In Chapter 1, "Be a Partner Not an Order Taker," we covered some scenarios and tools on how to make that transition. But that chapter is mainly a mindset, albeit a critical one for you to take the next step. In this chapter, we will dig deep into the implementation of behaviors that anchor the idea of partnership.

How do you provide feedback to others? For most people, it's a challenge, especially when they're trying to communicate with someone in an influential position. You may have a lot to say to your boss or your customer, but don't know how to say it. You may wait weeks or even months before getting up the nerve to say what's on your mind. But then you blow it. You're so wound up that when you finally speak, it comes off as whiny, petty, vindictive, or egotistical. Your feedback is flawed, and that's why the other person becomes defensive or angry when you offer it. Rather than helping the relationship, this type of feedback hurts it.

Or you may never provide any feedback at all. While you're civil and communicate the information the other person needs, you never go beyond the superficial issues. You never tell your boss or customer your feelings about the relationship and what might be done to make it more productive. You never point out problems that might help both of you be more effective in your jobs but also may involve some difficult conversations. Consequently, the relationship never advances to the next level, even though it may be perfectly amicable.

It is understandable that feedback is difficult to give. Your boss or your client has a direct impact on your compensation and your career. Why rock the boat? Why take a chance and tell him he's sabotaging a project with his recklessness? Why risk his anger by pointing out mistakes he's making? As difficult as it is to give feedback, giving feedback in a constructive way is even more difficult. Sometimes, when people start saying what's on their minds, their emotions get the better of them, and they go beyond feedback to emotional outbursts.

Offering feedback the right way is crucial if you want relationships that produce results. Trust that your honesty and insight will be valued if you understand what to say and how to say it. But you must overcome the natural reluctance to speak from your heart as well as your head.

THE ARGUMENT FOR FEEDBACK

I'm not going to tell you that giving a boss honest feedback is a pleasant experience, especially when you do it for the first time in the relationship. Expect to feel anxious; expect worst-case scenarios to run through your head. You're going to think of a million reasons to avoid telling your boss that his nitpicking is not just irritating but is interfering with the work.

In the same way, it's tough to control yourself when you do decide to be honest. All that pent-up anger and frustration can surface in many negative ways, including losing control of yourself because of passion, resentment, or not achieving results commensurate with your talent.

Leveling with a boss, a leader, a mentor, or anyone in a position of authority can seem counterintuitive, and fear of your message landing the wrong way may alter the manner and candor in which you deliver it.

All of this may deter you from offering honest and direct feedback. Don't allow that to happen. Force yourself to look at this issue from the other person's point of view. If you're in his shoes, do you want your direct report to sugarcoat the truth? Do you want your supplier to hold back key details because he's worried that revealing them might upset you? Of course not. You know you can't operate effectively if the other person isn't telling you everything you need to know.

When I'm speaking to groups about this subject, someone in the audience invariably raises her hand and says something to the effect of, "You don't know my boss." She goes on to explain how her boss is irrational, hot-tempered, overly critical, or just plain crazy. How can you be honest with a person like that?

If someone really is crazy or mean, and you've been working for him for a sustained period, I first pose the question, Why are you working for him? In further coaching and assessing, I've learned that most bosses and customers only appear this way. They may have gruff exteriors or be idiosyncratic, but they want to have a results-producing relationship as much as you do.

I have a client named Paul who is intimidating. He's a tough-talking New Yorker who can use sarcasm like a hammer. At one point, I decided that I needed to talk to him about my fee, which had not changed for two years. We had a good relationship, and I had done good work for Paul's organization, so it didn't seem out of bounds to at least raise the issue.

Nonetheless, I was anxious about broaching this subject. I worried that I might anger Paul to the point that he could fire me. I thought about how much easier it would be to play it safe—this was a big client, after all. And then I engaged in a self-dialogue that cleared my mind—and cleared the obstacles that I had put up between myself and Paul. What my self-dialogue boiled down to is the following reminder.

---

*We often say no to ourselves before we give the
other person a chance to say yes.*

After taking a few deep breaths, I walked into Paul's office for our meeting. We started by talking about other matters, and finally I said, "Paul, I was curious about how your budget looks for the coming year."

"Why," he snapped, "are you thinking of raising your fee?"

"Well, I was thinking of bringing up the subject for discussion to see what the opportunities were."

"You know, you're going to price yourself right out of this company."

Part of me wanted to stop right there and cut my losses. But a larger part knew that I had a valid point to make and wasn't going to rest until it was made.

"It's not my objective to price myself out of the company," I said. "My objective is keep your company as a client and continue to provide high value. But I'm a businessman, and I want to maximize the value I receive in return."

I'm not sure if it was what I said or how I said it—probably the combination—but I could see the effect of my words. Paul's features softened, he nodded slightly and asked what I had in mind. I gave him a figure, he came back with a lower one, and we arrived at a compromise number that struck me as eminently fair.

Providing direct and honest feedback isn't for the faint of heart. You need courage to sweep aside all the anxieties that cause you to shy away from these encounters. As the ol' cowboy, John Wayne said, "Courage is being scared to death but saddling up anyway."

As you may have guessed, offering straight talk to bosses and customers is linked to the lessons in Chapter 2, "Reveal Your Flaws without Fear." There has to be a give and take despite the fear both people in a relationship feel. This is the only way that relationships move to a higher level and produce the results you seek.

TIPS AND TECHNIQUES FOR LEVELING WITH A PERSON OF INFLUENCE

Your boss may provide you with plenty of feedback, but she probably won't invite you to return the favor. It isn't because she is not interest in hearing what you have to say, but because most of us have been conditioned to believe that feedback is a one-way street. If we're the boss or the client, we're the ones who tell others what we think of their performance.

Therefore, it is up to you to be the initiator. Make it your responsibility to tell your partner a difficult truth. Don't wait for her to say something first. Don't tell yourself it's not your place because you're in a "one-down" position managing up.

How you act, though, is key. If, for instance, I had been overly presumptuous or aggressive in my approach with my client, Paul, he would not have accepted my feedback. There are lots of good ways to provide feedback when you're managing up, over, and down. Here are three of the best tips to keep in mind:

1. Choose the right time.
2. Prepare and plan.
3. Align understanding.

Choose the Right Time

Bursting into your boss's office when he's racing to finish a project and then catch a plane isn't the best time to deliver feedback. Less obviously, approaching your boss or a client when she is distracted by a key, upcoming meeting or by a personal issue also isn't advisable. As eager as you might be to communicate your ideas or feelings, think about the timing issues in the following ways:

- *Identify the best time to approach a given individual.* This is not just identifying the worst times to avoid, but also knowing the periods when someone is most likely to be receptive to feedback. Determine if someone is a morning person or is in a better mood in the afternoon. Figure out his routines. When does he like taking breaks? When does he prefer to visit with people in his office (versus when he's usually too busy to visit)?

- *Ask "Is this a good time to meet?"* before beginning a feedback conversation. Give the person the opportunity to reschedule. Even if he has time when you ask, your question will have communicated that you're thinking about his schedule and not just your own issues.

- *Explain up front how much time you need.* This is an important conversation where you need the other individual's undivided attention. You don't want him to be looking at his watch every minute and making up an impending call or meeting. If there isn't sufficient time to say what you need to say and talk about it, reschedule.

- *Explain up front how important this conversation is.* Two things can happen if your boss or customers don't see the importance of the conversation. First, he may not give his full attention to what you have to say, and his responses may become perfunctory as a result. Second, he may figure he can placate you with a token nod of his head or by saying he understands. Unless he takes your words to heart, he's not going to respond in a way that ultimately leads to results.

- *Eliminate distractions.* I recognize that this isn't always easy. Your relationship partner may have a lot of responsibility and demands on his time. You don't control whether phones ring, computers signal incoming messages, or people barge in while you're sitting there. Nonetheless, you can attempt to minimize these distractions if not eliminate them. You can request that the other person hold his calls. Better yet, you can have the meeting in your office where you control the environment. Or you can schedule the discussion for lunch at a place that is quiet.

Prepare and Plan

Don't wing it. In the previous step, I suggested you communicate how important the meeting is. Communicate this same information to yourself. This isn't the time for ad hoc conversations. Put in some time and effort to figure out how you want the feedback conversation to go. Specifically:

- *Practice what you want to say.* Rehearse. Record or videotape your words. How do they sound? Does it seem like you're coming across as overly aggressive and accusatory? Or are you too meek and mild? The best tone is always confident, yet humble. It's generally wise to open a feedback discussion with a disarming question or statement, so think about how you might phrase one. For instance: "Do I have permission to speak honestly?" or "I've been thinking about something, but I hesitate to tell you because I'm worried about how you might respond."

- *Be succinct.* Don't ramble, but at the same time, don't speak so quickly that it seems like you can't wait to be done and out of there. Recognize that during that first feedback session, your anxiety may switch you to autopilot and cause you to speak a mile a minute. Adopt purposeful pausing, consciously keeping a measured pace as you deliver your message.

- *Suggest solutions rather than just raise problems.* Remember, feedback isn't only about saying what's wrong; it's about saying how things might be made right.

- *Be a professional.* This means controlling your emotions and presenting your feedback clearly and without histrionics. As much as your emotions may be roiling inside of you, remind yourself that you want people to focus on your message. If you're overly angry, upset, or frustrated, the other person will probably remember that, rather than what you said.

Align understanding

Many times, people deliver feedback as a speech rather than as part of a dialogue. Any time you offer feedback, there's the possibility of misinterpretation. For this reason, make an effort to determine if the other person in your relationship really *gets* what you're saying. You can do this in a number of ways, including:

- *Ask your relationship partner if she understands what you're trying to tell her.* You don't have to use words that suggest she's dense. Instead, use follow-up questions to probe her understanding. For instance, "Do you see why it bothers me when Joe bypasses me for these projects?" or "Does my frustration make sense to you, especially in light of how this has happened four times in the past month?" Refer to specific incidents that require the other person to address your feedback in detail rather than just providing a vague restatement of your concerns.

- *Clarify disconnects.* People misinterpret feedback all the time. Don't blame yourself. Communication is an imperfect art at best, and sometimes people hear what they want to hear. Don't panic when you realize that your boss or customer has drawn a conclusion that you absolutely didn't want her to draw. Instead, politely hold up your hand like a traffic cop and shake your head. Say something like, "I can see how you might think that, but it's not at all what I intended. What I really wanted to say is . . ."

- *Communicate what you hope the outcome of your feedback will be.* Ideally, your conversation should help you secure a commitment from your partner to respond to your feedback in a certain way. If you suggest that you're ready for more challenging assignments, you want her to acknowledge this fact and say that she is going to give you these assignments within the coming weeks. At the very least, by spelling out the results you find desirable, you will have given the other person a path to follow if she so chooses.

- *Get feedback on your feedback.* A large mistake most professionals make when giving feedback is they unwittingly approach encounters with a monologue approach. But in providing direct and honest feedback, you must be willing to solicit and receive it yourself. Open-ended questions like, "So what are your honest thoughts about my suggestions?" or "Do you have different insights that I may not be seeing?"

Remember, if you want others to be open-minded when you provide them with direct and honest feedback, you must practice the same behavior.

One additional tool that can make the feedback session pay off down the road is follow-up. Feedback is worthless if it's a one-time event. If you make giving feedback into a habit, it will make a difference in your job and your career. But, it's tough to do that. If you just get something off your chest, feel better, and aren't compelled to follow up; monitor what happens and offer feedback again. Checkpoint meetings should be regularly scheduled, mutually agreed upon conversations that revolve around perception. In other words, given the feedback, does each person perceive the situation in the same way? Have problems been resolved or does one person still believe problems exist? If during the initial feedback meeting, your boss agreed that you should be working on higher-level teams, do you feel your new team is the higher-level team you were talking about with your boss? Checkpoints help keep issues on track.

While checkpoint meetings have practical value, they also have relationship value; they represent a commitment to take feedback seriously and continually improve your own performance and that of those around you. People can respond positively to what you tell them, but unless they are committed to thinking long and hard about what you tell them, feedback will have little effect. When feedback is the regular cause for meeting and the subject of the meeting, it's elevated in importance.

I should also emphasize that performance reviews and other types of annual or semiannual appraisals are no substitute for checkpoints. Relationships are dynamic and evolve every day. If you save everything for one meeting at the end of the year, you're going to spend an inordinate number of hours hashing over old business—or you may not get to issues that are important, and instead focus on things that took place six months ago. These checkpoint meetings don't have to be long—a few minutes may be sufficient—but they need to take place at least once a month so that feedback is addressed continuously.

TROUBLESHOOTING: WHEN THE FEEDBACK SESSION DOESN'T GO AS YOU PLANNED

Being direct with a person of influence or power isn't always smooth sailing. Sometimes the other individual's reaction may hinder achieving your goal. People may be taken aback by your sudden candor. They may also feel threatened by what you're telling them; they may react defensively. In other instances, how you deliver the feedback may make this process more difficult than necessary. Everything from your tone of voice to your body language carries a message, and you may inadvertently be delivering that message in an off-putting way.

Whether it's you or the other person—or a combination of both—here are some common troubleshooting situations, followed by fixes you might try.

Scenario One

During your first feedback meeting, you attempt to be honest and open in your conversation with your relationship partner, but this person snaps at you. Despite your best intentions, you end up creating a further distance between your boss or client and yourself.

If this has happened to you, your first reaction may be to retreat. You want nothing to do with open and direct feedback ever again. It's a shock to have your words thrown back in your face. You think to yourself, "I tried to tell him the truth in a compassionate, straightforward manner, and all it did was make him angry." You tell yourself you're not going to put yourself in that place again.

But you need to go back there. The next time, try asking questions that might uncover the *why* behind his anger. You might say, "You seemed really angry the other day when I told you about x. Is there something going on that I don't know about?"

Never forget that even though the other person in your relationship is highly successful or seems incredibly confident and decisive, she's fallible, plagued by doubts, and not always certain what to do. Her surface reaction may be hiding a deeper pain, and it may have nothing to do with you. People are complex and emotional, and just because they are in positions of power doesn't mean they stop being human. Your boss may snap at you because your feedback hits a nerve; she's not mad at you but at herself for being weak or flawed in some way. This is a consistency I have witnessed at the highest levels of corporate cultures, even with the most successful of executives.

Give this person some time to gather herself, then come back to her and discuss why she became angry. The odds are that she calmed down and feels bad because she took her anger out on you. During your next encounter, she will be in a much more receptive mood for feedback and able to listen carefully to what you have to say.

Scenario Two

When you sit down and talk with the other person about your concerns, you find that you're greeted with nods and acknowledgments. You're being heard, but there is no action being taken. Your boss or client persists in the behavior that frustrated you to begin with, so it feels like he heard your feedback but doesn't care.

The odds are that the other person does care but doesn't realize how seriously bothered you are by what's been taking place. It's also possible that your boss was distracted by other matters and hasn't really focused on your feedback. Whatever the reason, the troubleshooting recommendation here is to practice "tactful persistence."

If you're married or in a serious personal relationship of any type, you've probably already used this tactic. You tell your spouse that this weekend you need to spend some time to shop for a new washing machine. Your spouse may not respond at first to this suggestion or may offer a flimsy excuse as to why he can't do it, but if you bring it up three or four times and do so tactfully, then it's likely that he'll do what you ask. Tactful, of course, is the key word. If you are unrelenting and aggressive in how you bring up the subject, it will come off as nagging, and you'll probably evoke a negative reaction.

Try introducing the topic of your feedback again in a different setting—over lunch instead of at the office, for instance. Try it again at a different time—the start of the day rather than at the end. Maintain a pleasant manner, but also communicate that this is a major issue for you and you don't want it to slip through the cracks. Face-to-face communication is the best approach, but if they are not responding, try a direct, succinct e-mail addressing your issues as well as your concern over their lack of response. Again, tactful persistence is key.

Scenario Three

You share your feedback with your relationship partner, but instead of responding to what you've said, she tells you what's wrong with your behavior/performance.

This isn't an exchange of direct and open feedback as much as an exchange of fire. Don't mistake feedback meetings for gripe sessions. You may have turned them into the latter by taking an accusatory stance. This may not have been your intent, but it's how you were perceived by the other person. Here are the three most common mistakes people make when they provide gripes instead of feedback:

1. Their tone is curt, hostile, or whiny.
2. They make it all about themselves. They don't phrase their complaint within the context of the relationship.
3. They don't listen to what the other person says.

If you think you may be guilty of any or all of these actions, here are four alternatives that should prevent your partner from responding with a volley of her own:

1. Adopt a pleasant but confident tone.
2. Talk about the issue from a collaborative perspective; explore what you can do together to resolve the issue.
3. Communicate that you're listening and valuing what you're hearing.
4. When you know they have a tendency to finish sentences and interrupt, begin the meeting by requesting, "I'd like to ask you to hear me out entirely for 90 seconds and then respond." Then get your point across in 90 seconds or within the time limit you requested.

BENEFITS: HOW FEEDBACK IMPACTS RELATIONSHIPS

Before addressing the specific benefits, I must remind you again that while I've emphasized the need for you to speak openly and honestly when managing up, you also must be receptive to the same straight talk from your boss or client. It's not just about you. The dynamic of two people providing each other with no-holds-barred insights is what elevates the relationship. When you give your boss permission to say anything to you, it helps you learn and grow, and when he grants you the same permission, the relationship benefits immeasurably. All self-censorship has been banished, and each person receives more value per conversation than seems possible.

With this mutual exchange of feedback in mind, let's look at some key relationship benefits:

- *Personal integrity*

Over the years, I've met people in organizations who may have had nice titles and been well-spoken, but they seemed more like actors than authentic people. They lacked a genuine quality. Instead, they were trying to fool others—and themselves—about who they were. They played a role and may have thought they were charismatic, but people viewed them as frauds. They may have believed they were wise and reflective, but their colleagues viewed them as overly cautious.

When people provide you with direct and honest feedback, it is difficult to continue to fool yourself. If you have a weakness or are missing a piece of knowledge or a skill, you have to face it and do something about it. You can't fake it. There's no hiding. As a result, this type of relationship forces you to be who you really are. And that's a powerful asset in any job or career. If you act in an authentic manner, people will respect you. You gain a certain authority by being true to who you are, and that often results in increased influence within a culture.

There's a poem written in 1934 by Dale Wimbrow called, "The Guy in the Glass," and its theme is that when you look at yourself in the mirror, that's how you'll be judged; that you gain strength of character when you can face yourself honestly. When you give someone feedback, and they do the same for you, then you are both winners. Or as the poem goes, "He's (the man in the mirror) the feller to please, never mind all the rest, / For he's with you clear up to the end, / And you've passed your most dangerous, difficult test / If the guy in the glass is your friend."

- *A free exchange of ideas and information*

When you're honest with someone about your thoughts and feelings, it's easy to be honest about everything from bad news to provocative ideas. In breakthrough relationships, people are extraordinarily well-informed. They make sure the other person is aware of all relevant events, trends, and changes within the organization.

- *A go-to resource*

You've heard the expression, "He's my right-hand man" (or right-hand woman)? It suggests that someone is indispensable; that this person can be relied on through thick and thin. When two people provide each other with direct and open feedback, each serves as the other's right-hand man. Feedback cements this tight relationship. Knowing that there is always someone you can count on to help when you get into trouble or are facing a great opportunity is a huge benefit, one that breeds loyalty, trust, and respect.

GETTING GREAT RESULTS

Let me end this chapter on feedback by telling you about Jack, the head of a midsize family business. When Jack took over the business from his father (who had recently died) at age 46, he hired an administrative assistant named Alice who was ten years his senior. Alice had worked in a similar capacity for a competitor for many years, but she was let go in a downsizing. At first, Jack felt lucky to have her simply because she knew the field backwards and forwards, and she was highly organized.

During his initial years as CEO, Jack was a bit lost. Though he had an MBA and had done well as an executive with a *Fortune 500* corporation, he had only been in the family business for five years and sometimes felt as if he were out of his element. While some of the employees were solid, some were long-time veterans who seemed to be coasting. Jack wasn't always sure if they were as informed about issues as they should be.

During the first few years with the company, Jack started telling Alice about a decision he was contemplating and asked her what she thought. Alice was a very strong-willed person who wouldn't mince words. She'd tell him if he was being overly analytical—one of Jack's flaws—or if he was too worried about hurting one of the veteran employees by making a certain decision. Jack found himself depending on Alice more and more, and after a while, he gave her the position of vice president, much to the consternation of some employees who resented that he was making a secretary an officer of the company.

For his part, Jack educated Alice about basic business management, an area where she had street smarts but lacked certain skills. Jack also helped Alice polish some of her rough edges. In an odd reversal of usual roles, Jack was shy about telling a woman ten years his senior, and who knew the industry much better than he did, that she needed to work on her presentation skills. After a while, though, Jack lost his hesitancy in speaking to Alice candidly. He explained to her that she was rubbing certain people the wrong way and that there were times when discretion was the better part of valor. He helped Alice keep in mind that there were certain situations where it was better to say nothing, than to say the wrong thing.

When Jack was 50 years old and Alice was 60 years old, he took on the title of chairman and made Alice his CEO. Not only did the company do better in the next seven years (until Alice retired) than it had ever done in the past, but Alice and Jack formed a great executive team that won the buy-in of even the most veteran employees as evidenced by the company's performance results.

In telling this story of Jack and Alice, I'm not saying that you should seek out your company's CEO, level with him, and expect that he'll adopt you as his heir. The morale of the story is that when people give each other strong feedback over time, the relationship is able to move to a level that it could never reach otherwise—a level that produces great results.

CHAPTER FOUR

Relish Productive Confrontations

For most people, confrontation is uncomfortable. In business, confronting a boss or customer is never easy. As you begin the process of developing partnering relationships, you may be concerned that confronting individuals with feedback may destroy the relationship. When you give honest and direct feedback to another person, you should anticipate some opposition. As the last chapter pointed out, the person you are providing feedback to may not agree with what you have to say. Rather than strengthening the relationship, making a simple observation about a relationship partner's recent decision can escalate into a confrontation about her management style. The good news is: that's not bad. The better news is: it could strengthen the relationship immeasurably.

If you're like most people, you manage up like you're handling a fragile piece of china. You believe that one argument might shatter the entire relationship; that if you disagree with your boss or customer, she'll think you're being difficult.

As uncomfortable as this confrontation may be, it is crucial to results-producing relationships. We all come from different backgrounds and have different perspectives, so if there isn't some friction in a relationship, someone isn't telling the truth. When people never debate or disagree, a false sense of harmony exists. Getting the truth out into the open is worth whatever discomfort you must endure. The best ideas often emerge from this truth—problem-solving, opportunity-seizing ideas. As strange as it may seem, disagreement, dissent, and debate are often the precursors to great revelations. Author Jim Collins of *Good to Great* (New York: HarperCollins, 2001) fame has said that he likes surrounding himself with people who challenge him and speak honestly, and I believe many leaders share this philosophy.

Unfortunately, the fear of negative consequences prevents people from confronting others, especially when those others are bosses, customers, or individuals in positions of influence. Some people are terrified that pointing out a problem in a relationship or challenging a boss on a key point will result in a huge fight, one that will permanently damage the relationship. Others fear that they don't have the right to confront, that their role as direct report or supplier mandates being agreeable rather than confrontational.

But the reality is that "productive confrontation" rarely harms a relationship and often strengthens it. I put those two words in quotes because it's a very different concept from ordinary conflict, and ensuring that your message is not perceived as simply confrontational is the key to making the exchange productive. If you challenge someone the wrong way—using the wrong words, tone of voice, or setting—then you could be compromising that relationship. No one likes a smart aleck, a bully, or a troublemaker. Even if your intent is positive, your message may come across the wrong way. Blurting out, "I disagree!" or storming into your boss's office and starting an argument is not productive and lacks professionalism and emotional intelligence.

The more conscious you are about how you confront others, the more results-producing such confrontations will be. The first step in raising your consciousness is drawing a clear distinction between productive confrontation and unproductive conflict.

DISAGREE WITHOUT BEING DISAGREEABLE

It's not just semantics. You can have a heated discussion with your boss about volatile issues and end up with a stronger relationship—and more effective solutions to solve problems—than you did before the discussion. It's not the heat that causes problems but the way you apply the heat. Let's say you believe your boss's decision to end a relationship with a supplier is the wrong one, and you decide to confront him about it. Here are two ways to do it.

Scenario One

As soon as you hear the news, you rush into your boss's office, point a finger at him, and say in a rushed tone of voice at almost twice your normal volume, "I can't believe you're firing Supplier A! I really hope this isn't another attempt to save a few pennies. We've been working with them for three years; they've always come through for us, and now we're dumping them. Is it because you don't like Joe? I always thought you didn't like him, but that's no reason to fire them."

Result: Your reputation is damaged. You are met with the same lack of respect that you showed in your approach, and future ideas from you might be given less consideration based on your handling of this single encounter.

Scenario Two

When you hear the news, you ask your boss if he has some time available this week to talk about Supplier A. You set up a time to meet later in the day, and when you enter his office, you sit down, exchange some small talk and then begin speaking in a calm, measured tone: "I was disappointed when I heard about Supplier A. And I'd like to share my opinion if that's all right? (Boss says 'Sure, go ahead.') I know that you and Joe have never gotten along well. I realize Joe can be difficult—I've had my problems with him also—but I wonder if we're making a mistake in cutting our ties with Supplier A because we've never had a supplier that has provided us with the service they have. And, if it helps, I will deal with Joe going forward and make certain we bring things to a more harmonious level. Thoughts?"

> *Result:* You make a strong statement in words, but a stronger one in approach because of your professionalism and diplomacy. Future decisions like this may not be made until your opinion is sought.

Unproductive Conflict versus Productive Confrontation

The differences between the unproductive conflict of the first example and the productive confrontation of the second may seem obvious, but it's worth spelling them out:

Unproductive Conflict

- Showing a lack of respect for the other person's motives or other priorities
- Offering one-sided intent; you only want to get your point of view across
- Using a loud voice and hostile body language
- Making the argument personal
- Bringing a win-lose mentality to the discussion

- Interrupting the other person before he can finish his sentences

Productive Confrontation

- Demonstrating respect for the other person's opinion and input
- Remaining open and interested in hearing what the other individual has to say
- Using a neutral tone of voice and body language
- Stating positions passionately and persuasively (but never angrily or accusingly)
- Bringing a win-win mindset to the discussion, with solutions and compromises as available options
- Making points directly and concisely
- Maintaining respectfulness and professionalism throughout the discussion

What lies behind these characteristics and determines whether you will have an unproductive conflict or productive confrontation is *attitude.* Some people consciously or unconsciously initiate conflict because they have a chip on their shoulders. In their interactions, they come across as angry, disrespectful, or whiny. People who confront productively are able to move past the anger, frustration, or other negative emotions they feel. They walk into their boss's office taking into consideration what their boss is thinking. They really want to understand how the boss arrived at a decision that seems wrongheaded. They're not there to debate or complain but to understand. And with that understanding, they hope to find common ground.

Finding Common Ground

I coached the CEO and CFO of a large company when they were struggling to maximize the results their relationship produced. Though they worked well together, they knew that if they could improve their relationship, they could work together at a more productive level. As they talked calmly and respectfully to each other about what might be holding them back, the CFO told the CEO that he was usually so glib and charming that it seemed like he only wanted to hear good news. "The reality is that things aren't always good," the CFO told him. "And every so often I really have to have a heart-to-heart talk with you, and I'm not sure you're ready to hear what I have to say."

The CEO was surprised by what the CFO was telling him, saying that he didn't realize that his positive attitude was having a negative effect on their relationship. He then added, "You know, you do have a doom-and-gloom attitude at times. I realize that your caution may come with the financial territory, but there are instances when it does bring me down, and I try to avoid you."

This exchange wasn't the perfect productive confrontation, at least as I define it. The discussion got a bit personal, and some anger crept into the exchange. But by and large, they were both respectful of each other, desirous of a win-win outcome, and direct and concise in their communication. As a result, they really listened to each other and began to understand their different viewpoints. The CEO grasped that the CFO's job is to protect the company from worse-case scenarios, so he's never going to be Mr. Positive. And the CFO came to realize that the CEO's *up* mood was critical to his leadership style, helping to inspire and motivate people through good times and bad.

At the end of the conversation, they reached an agreement: The CEO said he would not avoid the CFO on bad days, and the CFO said that when he had bad news to deliver, he would also come armed with potential solutions to or remedies for the bad news.

Although the CEO and CFO had worked together for 15 years prior to this conversation, this one meeting helped elevate their relationship to a level it had never achieved before. They began communicating more honestly, and this honest exchange resulted in finding better solutions to tough problems.

BUT WHAT IF . . .

When I advise clients to confront a colleague or boss, they always have a number of what-ifs that stand in their way. Let's look at some of the most common what-ifs and what you should do if they apply to your relationships.

What If the Confrontation Becomes Personal?

Slow the conversation down if you suspect it is heading in that direction. You need to monitor your own approach so you don't resort to accusations, whining, or defensive reactions. Similarly, if the other individual starts getting personal, you should try to steer the conversation back to the issue at hand. Admittedly, that isn't always easy, but if you don't respond in kind, most people will naturally gravitate back to the issue under discussion. Things get nasty when you're on the receiving end of accusations, and you only up the ante by responding with counteraccusations.

What If I Hurt the Other Person?

This is a surprisingly common fear whether you're managing up or down. Direct reports don't want to make their managers feel as if they're doing a bad job developing them. Suppliers don't want their customers to think they're being manipulated or pressured. In all of these situations, the individuals value their relationships and are concerned that confrontation will be a hurtful experience for the other person, perhaps even more than it will be for themselves.

To help diffuse potentially volatile exchanges, make your intention of the confronting conversation clear by saying something like, "I want us both to walk away with zero resentment and knowing that we can count on each other." Communicate from the very beginning that you want to maintain harmony and achieve a resolution of differences. A positive statement like this takes a lot of the sting out of what you have to say. It tells the other person that the confrontation is not just a one-sided list of complaints. Instead, your goal is to improve the relationship and assure that all parties walk away knowing that the meeting was time well spent.

What If Things Get Out of Hand?

The concern behind this question is that once you both get into it, the argument might become heated and one or both of you might say something you'll come to regret, which will damage the relationship. Confrontation is not always a rational, calm interaction. Things can get heated. But heat doesn't mean hurt. You can have a spirited disagreement without doing any damage to the relationship. You can both argue vociferously, be determined to state your case, and struggle to find a point of agreement. In some cases it is necessary to improve the relationship.

Things get challenging when the argument spirals out of control. When it turns into a heated win-lose battle or when one participant starts bad-mouthing the other or becomes stuck in past offenses ("Remember last year when you . . ."), then you are left with an unproductive conflict.

If a discussion begins to get off track, you can stop things from deteriorating further. Call a time-out if things become too tense. You can always say, "I don't think we're getting anywhere right now. Let's come back to this later in the week when I've had time to think about what you said." Without saying it, you're also asking the other person to think about what you had to say. Sometimes, this cooling off, reflective period allows the confrontation to resume on a calmer, less emotional level. Even if you both have used a tone or language that heated things up, time away from each other enables cooler heads to prevail when you reconvene.

What If the Other Person Isn't Receptive?

Most people *are* receptive, contrary to popular opinion. Despite people's fears that influential individuals have no interest in being confronted by those at lower levels, that simply isn't the case. At least it's not the case most of the time.

You may be in a professional relationship with individuals who just don't handle any sort of disagreement or debate well. These people may not even be conscious of their unapproachable attitudes, yet it is evident by their actions. For instance, one top executive in a company I worked with was a great visionary and extremely smart, but she lacked interpersonal skills. When she confronted her direct reports, she did so disrespectfully—she would embarrass and even humiliate them when she wasn't pleased with something they had done. She, on the other hand, was not interested in being confronted by any of her direct reports. A sign she pasted on her closed office door symbolized her resistance to confrontation: "NOT NOW!"

While it's true that people of influence are more accustomed to confronting rather than being confronted, the majority of executives do recognize the value of two-way confrontation. If they're confident and comfortable in their positions, they are receptive to people coming into their offices and objecting to their decisions or suggesting alternatives to their stated courses of action. They usually want to know if they're doing something wrong or if there's a more effective way to accomplish their objectives. And they prefer to know sooner rather than later.

To determine if your boss or client is receptive to confrontation, ask yourself the following:

- Is he self-confident; does he seem secure with who he is as a person and as a professional?
- Has she made it clear that she wants both the good news and the bad news; has she indicated that she's receptive to straight talk?
- Have you had disagreements or debates with this person in the past; have you observed others challenge this person; has the individual's response generally been positive?

PRODUCTIVE CONFRONTATION STEPS

While you may think that the most difficult individual to confront is the prototypical, ferocious boss, that isn't always the case. Confronting someone you like and respect is often more challenging than leveling with a difficult person; you're more worried about hurting someone's feelings when you care about them than when you have a more distant relationship them.

Productive confrontation isn't easy, no matter who it is you're confronting. The key to doing it well is having a process. If you plan what you are going to say and how you might respond to the other person in advance, you're going to handle the conversation better. To that end, here is a five-step process you can use to prepare yourself for a productive confrontation:

1. *Assess your own attitude and past behaviors regarding confrontation.*

The more aware you are of how confrontation friendly or averse you are, the smoother the confrontation will go. Think about past confrontations. Have you avoided them? When you've confronted or been confronted, have you become upset, defensive, furious, irrational, and so on? Do you tend to have problems confronting up though you do okay when confronting down? Don't rely only on your own perceptions. Ask colleagues and direct reports about your behaviors in these situations. Do they see you as someone who is good in confrontational scenarios? Or as someone who has problems with them? Do you not confront people because you want to be liked or have difficulty with disharmony?

Forewarned is forearmed. Just knowing your confrontation tendencies will clue you in on the obstacles you face when confronting someone and how a confrontational conversation might affect you. This awareness will help you plan your strategy. If, for instance, you know that you tend to back off at the first sign of resistance or anger from the other person, then you can rehearse what you might say if you encounter this reaction.

- *Engage in self-talk based on your assessment.*

Talk to yourself about your confrontation tendencies. Consider why you act the way you do and why you might want to act differently next time. Zero in on your planned confrontation. Ask yourself what the potential consequences are if you speak your mind . . . and what the consequences are if you remain silent. In certain situations, silence may be the loudest voice you have. More often than not, though, this self-talk will motivate you to take action. Typically, the consequences for speaking out are more positive than the consequences for remaining silent.

- *Test their expectations and create rules of engagement.*

Do you know how to eat an elephant? One bite at a time so the elephant doesn't squash you. In other words, move forward methodically. Ideally, you'll have the opportunity prior to the confrontation to scope out how your relationship partner deals with confrontation. If you don't know, test them by asking a few questions: "When I'm concerned about something and need to have a heart-to-heart discussion with you, what is the best time and place to do so?" or "When things get hot, and I have a problem with something you say or do are you open to feedback?" You should test their expectations regarding confrontation.

Based on these expectations, you can set some rules. For instance, you both expect the other person to be straightforward without being accusatory. If the conversation becomes too hot, you can call a time-out and reschedule it for the following week.

- *Confront honestly, empathetically, and professionally.*

Keep these three adverbs in mind during your conversation. They will help you maintain the delicate balance between stating your own beliefs and being aware of the other person's sensitivities and reactions. It's a delicate balance because you want to be forthright, but you also want to be respectful of your colleagues' needs, values, and requirements. For instance, let's say you go into a client's office and protest about a new requirement he's imposing on you. You don't feel it's necessary, and you make that point clear. He responds that his hands are tied, that it's a new company policy that applies to all consultants. You go back and forth on the issue, but he keeps repeating the same point and refuses to give in. At that point, the honest, empathetic, and professional way to respond is, "Okay, I can see what you're saying, and you're not giving in. So is this the end of the discussion? Or, is there something I can do that might help influence your company to change the policy as it regards us? Or would it be useful to bring this up with you again in another month?"

Recently, Calvin, one of my partners at Victory Consulting, and I had dinner with a client CEO named Charlie. The two had been working together in a successful coaching program for almost a year. But Calvin thought their working relationship and professional outcomes could be moved to a more productive level. To that end, right after dinner he said to Charlie, "You know, there are times when I want to give you honest feedback, but when things get heated, you tend to respond in a dismissive way, so I'm hesitant to give you the feedback I think you should hear." Charlie expressed to Calvin that he was surprised to hear this. Calvin said, "Well, your body language reinforces this impression. We tend to lose eye contact at these moments, and you kind of turn away from me and busy yourself with something on your desk." The CEO told him, "I relish honest feedback. So the next time I do this, ignore it, and feel free to speak your mind." Simply making Charlie aware of this has escalated their respect and business results to a more powerful level.

- *Try to get to the why behind the what.*

Too many confrontations get bogged down in the *what* of a situation. You tell your boss the specific things he does that bother you, and he responds with a recap of what you did to cause him to take these actions. This is fine, but it doesn't go far enough. You need to probe why your boss did what he did, and you need to explain your rationale as well. The *why* is where the real opportunity for improving a relationship can be found. Once you know why your customer treated you the way he did, it might make sense. Once you understand the other person's motivations, you might empathize with them and realize that your reason for confronting no longer exists. We're very quick to assume the *why* behind the *what,* but our assumptions aren't always accurate. We assume our boss didn't give us the big assignment because of something unfounded, while in truth, he has a logical reason for withholding it.

DO YOU WANT WITNESSES?

In the majority of situations, confrontation works best when it's done one-on-one. When you have privacy, you don't have to worry about embarrassing the other person in front of others; you also don't have to worry about embarrassing yourself. It's generally easier to be honest and straightforward when you don't have an audience. A one-on-one exchange also promotes the type of dialogue that can strengthen the relationship. You can talk about delicate issues that you may have avoided in the past, going in depth about thoughts and viewpoints you may never have broached before. This is great stuff, and you should take advantage of it through a one-on-one exchange.

But there are also times when confronting an individual within a group is more appropriate. Sometimes, this isn't even a matter of consideration—you don't have a choice. One client I work with, Tony, is the president of a large construction company. Tony had been meeting with a representative from a hospital group about building a new hospital. He and the rep had established a good relationship, the deal had just about been sealed, and the rep invited Tony and his team to present their plan to his hospital team.

During the presentation, the rep began asking Tony's team questions that challenged their experience and building methodology. Tony found the questions insulting. He and the rep had already addressed all these issues in their previous, private meetings, and they had done so in a collaborative manner. The rep seemed as if he were putting on a show for his selection committee, demonstrating his toughness and foresight. Finally, Tony had enough. He stood up and said, "I thought we were going to be partners, that we both wanted to collaborate and build something great. Clearly, all you want to do is poke holes in what we plan to do."

With that, Tony asked his team to stand and walk out with him.

The hospital rep was shocked and taken aback, and he quickly apologized. He said that he wanted to challenge each team but did not intend to offend any of the contractors. Shortly after things settled down, the presentation resumed with a tone of mutual respect. Three days later, Tony's group was awarded the new hospital building job, and the rep and Tony enjoyed an increasingly solid relationship over the next few years.

While I'm not suggesting that you confront your clients in this manner, this story illustrates one use of group confrontation. Tony was put in a situation where he needed to speak out and confront—he and his team were embarrassed in front of the hospital board, and he had to assert strength by confronting the rep. The rep was a decent person who made a mistake, and Tony was pointing out that mistake in a dramatic manner. No doubt, if the rep weren't a good person, he might have pulled the job from Tony out of spite. The rep may not have approved of Tony's actions, but he understood his own actions had precipitated them. When Tony challenged him in public, the action communicated to everyone that if he wanted to continue the relationship, this behavior would not be tolerated. The group confrontation drove the point home in a way that would not have had the same impact if had been carried out in a one-on-one meeting.

When you confront within a group, the witnesses tend to amplify your words. Something that you say in private might not get through to them; they tune you out, consciously or unconsciously. In a group setting, this is more difficult to do because of the additional pairs of ears.

It's difficult to ignore a public utterance because it's now a matter of public record.

These witnessed confrontations can help define a relationship, but they may come with a cost. As I noted earlier, Tony's hospital rep might have responded to the confrontation by ending the relationship. That's a risk that he felt was worth taking. Within a given relationship, you reach a point where you need to make a bold statement about what's acceptable and what's not. Of course, it is vital to give a lot of thought to when, where, and with whom you make this statement—it's a technique to be used judiciously. Like Tony, you may be placed in a situation where all your instincts tell you to confront now in public rather than later in private.

DEALING DIRECTLY WITH DIFFICULT ISSUES

While confrontation can have a profound effect on how two people interact, constant confrontation, like continuous consensus, isn't healthy for a relationship. It can be taxing on both parties if you're always arguing about issues and challenging the other person to do something better or different. But when you give and receive permission to confront—when it's accepted as part of the relationship— you save time, increase your productivity, and accomplish your goals. Why? Because confrontation cuts to the chase. Instead of dancing around sensitive issues or ignoring them altogether, you and your relationship partner deal with them head-on. A certain amount of confrontation also earns the confronter respect.

For example, Lois was a senior manager within a large bank, and on a Monday she and coworkers came into the office to discover that the company had done work on their cubicle area—erecting a wall that blocked the natural light that came through the windows where her team worked. Needless to say, Lois and her direct reports were not happy about this wall. She decided to say something about it to Terri, who was assistant to the president and in charge of office décor.

Lois started out by telling Terri that she and her colleagues felt slighted because they weren't consulted or even advised about the wall. She explained that it not only reduced the natural light in their cubicles but effectively divided some of the members who worked on the same team. Lois also mentioned that the barrier would impede communication with half of her coworkers and make it more difficult for them to collaborate on projects.

Terri said she understood that Lois was unhappy, but that they needed to hire new staff members and that the wall partition was part of the plan to add more office space.

"You know, this wall doesn't really affect you," Lois said. "No disrespect to the new staff members, but as a veteran of this company, I would at least expect to be consulted about something that impacts my team and their work environment. If someone did talk to me, I would tell her that open space is an important component in how our department communicates and also how we feel when we are working."

Initially, Terri was a bit put off by the confrontation, but after thinking about what Lois said and talking to other people who worked in the area, she realized that Lois was making some valid points and realized that taking action before consulting Lois had been a bad move. Perhaps most significantly, the experience created a relationship between Lois and Terri that before had barely existed.

Your confrontations may be nothing like the one just described. They come in all shapes and sizes, from controlled, professional debates to emotionally wrenching dialogues. They can last a few seconds or go on for hours or even go on serially for days or weeks. They can focus on the same issue or issues or they can cover a variety of topics.

*The confrontation topic doesn't matter as much as
the way it's handled by both parties.*

If you want to realize better results, then it's critical to exert control over confrontations and to do so with kindfidence. Keep them as short and as sweet as possible. Make them businesslike discussions, but do your best to go in with a resolute optimism so that both parties win. Easier said than done, but concentrate on what's important to the other person as you talk about the issue. In this way, you're going to communicate more than just complain. You're going to demonstrate your perceptivity and your understanding of the other person. In this way, the confrontation will lead to a stronger relationship that builds trust and performance while avoiding the negatives of unproductive conflict.

CHAPTER FIVE
Make Gratitude a Habit

Can you compliment as well as confront? It is essential to have the courage to level with your boss or your customers. But it's just as important to express your appreciation. Oddly, some people are better at confronting than thanking. They don't want to be perceived as suck-ups, or they find it awkward to articulate their appreciation. They rationalize this attitude, telling themselves that their boss, colleagues, or direct reports don't need to be thanked because they may already receive plenty of kudos from others.

> *"The deepest principle in human nature is the craving to be appreciated."*
>
> —William James

We all need to be appreciated, as quoted by American psychologist and philosopher, William James. Even the most powerful, accomplished business leaders possess this same craving, and it persists even when they have been lauded by a national business publication, win awards, or receive seven-figure salaries. They still hope and expect that their direct reports will communicate how much they appreciated a raise or promotion. Similarly, when people aren't appreciated, resentment, disconnection, and loss of loyalty may result over time. More people leave organizations because they feel unappreciated than for any other reason.

Of course, we don't all like being appreciated in the same way. At one extreme, some people crave constant flattery. At the other extreme, they prefer subtle, low-key expressions of appreciation. Knowing how to tailor your gratitude in different situations for different individuals is key, and these methods will be explained here. First, I'd like to illustrate how appreciation impacts relationships by sharing two scenarios with you.

A SIMPLE THANKS WILL DO, AND A WRITTEN THANKS MAY DO BETTER

John is a project manager and a junior partner in a large construction company, and he just completed a $125 million dormitory for a client before the deadline and under budget. It was a challenging project, and John worked long hours and came up with a creative approach to make sure the project moved forward without a hitch. As always, John worked well with both the client and his own team. Polite, always on time, smart, talented, and generous in giving credit, John is a valuable member of the firm, and his excellent qualities were especially useful on this project.

When the dormitory was completed, John's senior partner, Mark, never expressed his gratitude for all of John's hard work. Mark met with John shortly after the project was completed, told him *the client was happy*, but never said one word about his own appreciation for John's efforts. Instead, he simply discussed John's next assignment and then told him that he was late for a meeting and would see him later in the day.

John was furious when he left Mark's office. He thought to himself, "This is BS! I gave my all to get the project completed. The client and my staff are happy with the results, the firm just made a lot of money, and Mark acts like it was no big deal? That's it! If Mark doesn't appreciate what I've done now, he's never going to appreciate my work. I'm tired of being taken for granted. Tomorrow, I start looking for a new job."

Now consider an alternate scenario, one in which everything remains the same: John does a good job on the project, Mark doesn't immediately express appreciation. In this case, however, Mark recognizes that he needs to overcome his reluctance to express gratitude. He can't bring himself to do it verbally, so he writes the following letter:

> John,
>
> Congratulations on leading our company successfully on this very important project. Our client loves us, the project team is ecstatic, and you are the catalyst for these accomplishments.
>
> I've been in this business for more than 30 years and can honestly say you are one of the best young managers I've worked with. Your enthusiasm and attitude are contagious. Your work ethic and candor create trust and build morale. Most of all, you take time to keep everyone abreast of what is going on and how they contribute. All of these are not just traits of an exemplary leader but the sign of a winner.
>
> Keep up the good work and thanks for your efforts. We're proud to have you as a member of this company.
>
> Mark

The odds are that John would not be considering quitting his job in this second scenario. A sincere, heartfelt expression of gratitude makes you want to continue working with and building the relationship with the person who offered you this praise. At the very least, it gives you pause about looking anywhere else for a job.

Though Mark was essentially managing down in this scenario, the two contrasting approaches illustrate how much of a difference a single expression of gratitude can make in a relationship. And if one expression can make a difference, results are the inevitable reward of expressing gratitude consistently.

DOS AND DON'TS

By definition, expressing gratitude is personal, so it shouldn't be done in cookie-cutter fashion. Like Mark, you may find it easier to use writing to say thanks. In addition, you have to consider the other person and how he or she might respond to a certain type of expression. Some people are embarrassed when they receive too much praise for something they've done. Or they don't expect to be thanked for the little things—they just want appreciation shown when they've made a significant effort on someone's behalf.

Because of all these variations, there is no definitive way to express gratitude effectively. There are however, some basic guidelines that will serve you well no matter who you are or the type of person your relationship partner is. Consider the following Dos and Don'ts:

Do

- Use a sincere tone of voice.
- Use the person's name while communicating.
- Employ handwritten expressions of gratitude around the "why."
- Be specific in noting the behaviors and traits for which you're grateful.
- Use body language (direct eye contact, smiles) to communicate your appreciation.

- Be concise in your expression.
- Say what you mean and mean what you say (be honest and express that honesty with feeling).

Don't

- Offer appreciation using a neutral or disinterested tone of voice.
- Qualify your gratitude with negative comments or use it to ask for favors.
- Be abrupt or grudging in the way you express appreciation.
- Brag about your own accomplishments while you are complimenting someone else.
- Diminish your appreciation by communicating it in a quick e-mail or as an offhand remark.
- Turn your gratitude into a joke by being sarcastic or making fun of an accomplishment.

We've all committed some of these don'ts in certain situations, so the goal isn't to be perfect in your expression of gratitude. But as you review both lists, ask yourself if you're more likely to commit the dos or the don'ts. Some people find it difficult to offer a genuine compliment without turning it into a joke—they feel uncomfortable sincerely communicating their thanks. Others see gratitude as a tool to help them get what they want. Marilyn tells her boss what a great job he did in dealing with a customer's request for additional services; that she really admires how he spent so much time and effort meeting the customer's requirements. Then Marilyn adds, "I know we have an upcoming project with Client X. I think I could really help ease your workload if you let me work on it with you."

Not only does this approach water down the expression of appreciation, but also, the motivation for it is transparent.

It's the same trick kids use when they want something from parents: "Oh Mom, you really look great tonight. And can I go to a party at Billy's house?"

One of the most important things to remember is to be specific. That's because generalized comments are a dime a dozen. If you tell your customer, "Thanks for helping us out today," after he goes to bat for your firm with his management team, it's like saying, "Thanks for holding the door open." Not bad, but not memorable either. If, on the other hand, you say, "Joan, I really want to thank you on behalf of my entire team. I know it might have been difficult for you to defend our firm in front of Tom since he's been skeptical of our abilities because we're a small firm. But, I'm sure you won him and the other management team members over by citing those three projects we handled in the last year, and how each one of them exceeded the goals you set. You really made a difference, and it's truly appreciated."

Also important is saying thanks holistically. In other words, don't just say thanks, but express gratitude with your tone of voice, your eyes, and even your posture. Maybe you don't notice it, but people are affected not just by your words but also by the look in your eyes, by how you hold yourself, and by the warmth in your voice. You can deliver a powerful expression of appreciation when all these elements are working together. You send the message that your appreciation is heartfelt. This makes a lasting impression on people, cementing and strengthening relationships in ways that other behaviors can't. People remember these deep expressions of gratitude because they don't happen that often. I'm not telling you to give a five-minute, impassioned speech to your boss about how grateful you are that he gave you the weekend off. I am suggesting that when you are truly grateful for something your relationship partner did, express it fully rather than halfheartedly.

How often you communicate your appreciation is partly situational and partly personal style (and ego). The dos and don'ts vary based on what your relationship partner has done for you—you don't want to express gratitude for something trivial or something that doesn't really deserve thanks. And you don't want to be inauthentic when you communicate your appreciation. If your style is low key, you don't want to gush your thanks. Consider your natural way of saying thanks and use that genuine approach.

And here's one final do: ask for feedback from others about how you express gratitude. This is an area where people can fool themselves. I know one business executive who is convinced that he regularly thanks people for their help, and in reality, he is known as someone who seems cold and ungrateful for assistance. It is likely that this executive truly believes he is good at thanking others. In his mind, he remembers telling people thank you for this. What he doesn't remember is that when he said thank you, he made a sarcastic joke that negated his appreciation, or that he didn't look someone in the eye when he told her he appreciated her help.

Obtaining feedback from colleagues as well as friends can help ensure your intentions and the results are aligned. Ask them if you are someone who regularly expresses appreciation sincerely. *Regularly* and *sincerely* are key words. If you say thanks once in a blue moon, that's not going to help you form a results-producing relationship. In the same way, if you express gratitude with a chip on your shoulder or with clear reluctance, it's not going to do any relationship much good. Pay attention to what people tell you about your gratitude attitude. If you hear you're generally ungrateful or inconsistent in your expressions, then work on it.

MODES OF EXPRESSION

Tim had a terrific mentor who had helped him enormously over the years, but he said that he had thanked him so many times for his assistance that he felt like he was overdoing it; that it was more like a routine than a sincere thank-you. I suggested that Tim try something different in addition to his face-to-face communication—why not buy his mentor a gift? And instead of saying thank-you in person every time his mentor helped him, he could use the phone on certain occasions or send a note. In this way, these varied expressions of gratitude feel fresher and more honest.

Besides face-to-face interactions, here are some different modes of expression you might consider:

- *Call on the phone.* Phone calls are less personal than face-to-face meetings, but they are good supplements to such meetings. Perhaps you use the phone to reiterate how much you appreciate something: "I'm just calling to tell you that helping me deal with those guys in finance was really great, and I don't want you to think that I don't appreciate what you did."

- *Use e-mail, handwritten notes, and cards (that you personalize) to formalize your appreciation.* Putting something in writing tends to make it more memorable. Writing allows you to communicate things that you might not be able to articulate as well verbally. Potentially, it is a more considered, eloquent expression of appreciation that will have greater meaning than anything you might say, particularly if it's handwritten rather than typed on the computer.

- *Buy a gift.* This is a mode of expression to be used selectively. Reserve it for special occasions, such as a boss giving you a promotion or a customer selecting your firm for a big new piece of business. Make sure the gift is appropriate. If it's too expensive, it may seem like a bribe or a payoff. If it's too cheap, it may feel like a token gift. Use the same philosophy that guides your personal gift giving: Figure out what the other person really likes, doesn't have too much of, and will really use or enjoy. For a baseball fan, it might be tickets to a game. For a wine lover, it might be a bottle of his favorite type of wine. Gifts are always symbols of appreciation, so choose your symbol appropriately and do a little homework and background investigation to discover the right ones.

- *Give a hug or pat on the back.* Again, you need to be appropriate. Some people don't like to be hugged or touched by their colleagues. Others can get the wrong idea from physical contact. Most of the time, however, these gestures are subtle but significant ways to establish stronger connections with people. They demonstrate that you view what you're saying as more than just words.

- *Treat them to lunch.* Too often, a boss or customer takes you out to lunch, and you don't reciprocate. It seems to be the thing to do when you're managing down rather than managing up. In reality, it's probably a more significant gesture when you're managing up, just because it's not the norm. You don't have to take someone to the fanciest place in town, but you should choose a place you think the other person will like. An appreciation lunch also gives you a more relaxed environment to explain why you are grateful for the help.

Saying thank you is an art, and you should use all the art forms at your disposal.

THE SUCK-UP OBSTACLE

If you are managing up, you may be worried about expressing gratitude for fear of coming across like a yes-man (or yes-woman). You've probably observed others who buttered

up their bosses to secure promotions or favorable treatment, and you don't want to be perceived as fawning. As
a result, you make a conscious effort not to compliment
bosses, believing that it's better to maintain your integrity.
The same concerns can apply to the relationship between
business owners and their customers; we don't want
our customers to feel we are being less than genuine in our
appreciation of them.

You can maintain your integrity as long as you're honest about how you express appreciation. If you go into
your boss's office angling for a raise and telling her what
a terrific manager and leader she is, then you're clearly
using gratitude as leverage to get what you want. In these
instances, you will be perceived as manipulative, obsequi-
ous, and other negative things.

Even if you don't have any specific intent in complimenting or thanking someone with influence, you need to
be conscious of your timing. If you find yourself expressing gratitude to people just when you need their help with
something, then your compliments may be unconsciously
articulated with ulterior motives. If you know a customer is about to decide whether to give your firm a big
new assignment, sending him a handwritten note detailing what a wonderful person he is to work with may cause
him to view your gesture negatively. So be careful about
your timing to avoid the perception of being crass and
manipulative.

Similarly, pay attention to how effusive you are in
your expressions of gratitude. Ask yourself, "Is my thank-
you right in terms of content and style, given the situation?" If you go on and on about how wonderful your boss
is because he gave you a day off, then you're overdoing it.
Similarly, using superlatives ("You're the best client I've
ever had"), being melodramatic, ("Your stellar presentation
saved the account!"), or using any type of hyperbole creates
an impression of insincerity. You may be completely sincere,

but your over-the-top performance makes other people suspicious about your motives.

Evaluate your motivations by asking yourself a few key questions after an interaction when you offer someone a compliment or express thanks. Specifically:

- Why did you say what you said, was it primarily for the other person or for yourself?
- What were you really hoping to communicate: your appreciation for the other person or some other agenda related to your job goals?
- Did you express your appreciation from the heart, guided by your head (saying what you believed) or from the head, with a touch of heart (consciously trying to show you were sincere, even if you were not)?

These questions, asked repeatedly over time, will help you become more aware of your motivation and guard against expressing gratitude with hidden agendas, which may even be consciously hidden from you. In most instances, people who are viewed as suck-ups are those who are obviously insincere in their behavior. If you are genuine in how you express appreciation and compliments, it really won't matter how it appears to others. The person on the receiving end will recognize that your expression was authentic, and it will help create a stronger, more productive relationship.

WHAT SHOULD I EXPRESS APPRECIATION ABOUT?

This question might seem obvious, but many times, people are at a loss about what they should thank others for consistently. They know to say thank you when their boss gives them a big raise or when a customer provides them with a great referral, but they fail to see the wide variety of reasons that call for appreciation.

To help raise your awareness of when you can and should say thank you, do the following exercise:

> At the top of a piece of paper, write the names of two respected work colleagues. Then take two minutes to list all the qualities you admire in each person. Total the number of qualities listed for each.
>
> Then answer these questions: During the past few months, have you expressed your appreciation for any of these qualities to either person; how many of the qualities did you express appreciation for?
>
> Next, translate a specific quality into a statement of gratitude. For instance: "Courageous. I appreciated the courage you demonstrated last week when you explained to the CEO that our group couldn't reach our objectives unless the budget was increased."
>
> Make a commitment to express this statement within the next week.

For most people, this exercise opens their eyes to the disconnect between how much they appreciate the qualities of their colleagues and how infrequently they share this appreciation. It also gives them a method to translate their admiration into appreciative behaviors.

If you find yourself struggling with the translation part of the exercise, try thinking in terms of specific, recent events— a meeting, a presentation, or a conference—and whether the person in question exhibited this quality in a situation where you were involved or were merely an observer. To express gratitude, it helps to have a specific, recent instance in mind.

Beyond this exercise, you should think about all the different reasons you might express gratitude. Many times, we limit our thinking to monetary issues—raises, bonuses, lucrative new business assignments, and so on. Certainly, if someone helps you achieve greater financial success, you should express your gratitude. But there are many other areas you should consider. Here are some examples:

- *Mediating a conflict between you and a colleague:* Personality conflicts are common in any work setting, and they can simmer and boil over, causing both parties a lot of problems. Mediating conflicts between people is often a thankless task, so you should say thank you if your relationship partner takes on this task.

- *Providing you with a great project:* Challenging or stretch assignments are not always easy to obtain. If your boss or your boss's boss helped you get one, someone was thinking highly of you. Expressing gratitude in return makes everyone feel good, while generating bottom-line business benefits for your relationships.

- *Helping you learn something new:* A boss or customer may teach you a new skill or help you become proficient in a new area, but whatever the learning involves, it takes time and effort to impart it. In an era where knowledge management is critical, anyone who helps you learn is worthy of gratitude.

- *Assisting you with help on a project:* You may be facing a tight deadline or have run out of ideas about how to solve a problem. When your colleague is willing to pitch in and give you assistance with a project, you should be grateful. Many people let their direct reports sink or swim, and if your boss is willing to rescue you and come up with a problem-solving idea or contribute his time to meet a deadline, then you should express appreciation.

- *Offering career advice:* This goes beyond the call of duty for most bosses and customers. Not only is there no immediate payoff for them in offering this advice, but also it could result in you finding a better job elsewhere. If they draw on their years of experience and wisdom to give you some tips about your career path and long-term goals, tell them how much this advice means to you.

INFUSING RELATIONSHIPS WITH TRUST, LOYALTY, AND GOODWILL

Expressing gratitude without attitude is a nice thing to do, but it's also an action that has a relationship payoff. The practice of showing gratitude is about more than just being a polite or decent human being. Relationships that produce results depend on a gratitude exchange—on both parties telling each other when the other has exhibited compassion, intelligence, courage, selflessness, and so on. If gratitude is exchanged consistently and honestly over time, it produces three relationship effects:

1. *Higher levels of trust*

Think about what happens when someone tells you how much he appreciates the effort you make on his behalf. It doesn't have to be a work experience, but this expression could have taken place at any time in your personal life. Maybe it was a sibling or a friend thanking you for something you did—helping this individual study for a test or recommending him for a job. I would bet anything it made you feel that the other person really valued you because he was willing to admit that he was in your debt for the effort you made on his behalf. I would also bet that it made you more willing to express your appreciation to him when he did something magnanimous. No doubt, he also felt that you valued him. When both people in a professional relationship place high value on each other, it facilitates trust.

2. *Greater loyalty*

You may be loyal to your boss or your customer, but you may not be certain the reverse is true. When you're managing up, you need to build the relationship to a point where the other person believes you're someone to whom he should be loyal. More than one customer believes their vendor only values them because of the business they give that vendor's firm. More than one boss believes that a direct report only cares about them because they control that direct report's compensation and movement upward through the company. The bosses assume that the direct report would take another job at a different company for more money, and the customers believe the vendor would switch to a new customer if it gave his firm more business.

I'm painting a cynical picture to make a point: you need to earn loyalty. Give your relationship partners a reason to believe you're in it for more than the money. When you express gratitude consistently and honestly, you provide that reason, whether you are communicating it upward, downward, inside, or outside your organization.

3. *Goodwill*

Recognition, acknowledgment, and gratitude make people want to work together. Too often, business relationships are products of convenience rather than of good feelings. It's about process, not people; yet process does not work without people. We don't work together because we're assigned to do so. We may get along okay and work productively, but we don't particularly enjoy it or get much out of relationships. As a result, we are less willing to do much for one another beyond what is expected, and there is no sense of team in the work.

Expressing gratitude the right way can make our relationships more productive and rewarding. Most relationships are transactional; they lack an emotional bond. When a gratitude exchange is the relationship norm, it creates a bond. When good feelings exist, people want to go the extra mile for their partners.

Above all else, expressing gratitude frequently and authentically makes relationship partners want to do more for each other. It's the gasoline for higher performance. When you know the other person truly appreciates your efforts on his behalf, he will want to do even more than he did before. You are confident that you'll be rewarded both with his gratitude and with his reciprocal effort on your behalf.

CHAPTER SIX

Become an Exceptional Listener

Question: If you don't listen to the goals of others, how can you win the highest results from them; build trust, performance, and profit; and help them reach those goals?

Answer: You can't. Listening requires knowledge, selflessness, and practice.

In my experience, exceptional listening is rare, while poor listening is common. The best listeners are usually the greatest leaders, salespeople, mentors, coaches, parents, and friends. What is required to be an exceptional listener? Read on.

A decade ago, I met a 25-year-old woman named Mary Hepburn. I've never met anyone who listened to people as unconditionally and without judgment. When people spoke to her, she gave them her undivided attention. From her fully-engaged focus to the way she responded with just the right question or expression when you spoke, it was very clear that she was interested in what you were saying rather than in how a conversation might benefit her.

I have been bragging to audiences about Mary since first meeting her. People often ask me, "Why is she the best listener you've met?" They challenge my assertion saying, "I listen with empathy and without judging. I'll bet I've heard every word you've said."

At this point, I offer a very simple distinction: Mary Hepburn is deaf, but still an extraordinary listener.

Hearing is the ability to perceive sound. Listening is the execution of great communication.

When you truly listen to what someone is saying—when your head and heart are fully involved in the exchange—you are doing much more than hearing what someone has to say. When you listen deeply, you're fulfilling a need that everyone has. People want sincere appreciation for what they have to say. Relationships rise and fall on the ability to communicate sincere appreciation, and it all starts with genuine, fully engaged listening.

When you listen, do you communicate that you care about the person who is speaking, that you value his ideas, and that you are fully engaged in the conversation? When answering that question, consider the most common mistakes of individuals who don't listen well.

FOUR SINS OF BAD LISTENERS

Hearing without listening happens all the time in business relationships. At some point, we've all been guilty of it. Maybe we're preoccupied with another matter and don't really pay attention to what someone is saying. At times, we become so excited about what we have to say that our excitement drowns that person out. There are instances when we're anxious because we don't feel prepared and so we feign listening, and try to convince a boss or customer that we were paying attention.

Just because this is a scenario we can all relate to doesn't mean we have to make a habit out of it.

Being conscious of listening habits means questioning your-self regularly about whether you're paying attention with your whole being. Most of us listen at about a 25 percent capacity, even in important business situations with those who can influence our outcomes. You would think that we would be all ears when influential partners are speaking, but that often isn't the case. We know we can get by if we listen with one part of our mind while the other parts are thinking about whether a deadline can be met, if an e-mail response arrived yet, and what we might have for dinner.

To help improve your listening skills, keep these fol-lowing four sins in mind:

1. The interrupter
2. The sentence finisher
3. The friendly faker
4. The rehearser

The Interrupter

Frequently interrupting others when they are speaking sends a negative message: "I really am not interested in paying attention to what you have to say, which is why I'm not allowing you to finish your sentence and telling you what I think instead—obviously what I have to say is more important than what you're saying."

While you don't intend to communicate this idea to a client or supervisor when you interrupt, that is the mes-sage you send by interrupting. The problem is that we often think we have good reasons to interrupt. Think back to a recent instance when you interrupted someone at work. Did you do so because:

- The other person said something that energized you, and you just couldn't wait to contribute your idea?

- You disagreed with the other person and were so angry or disturbed by his position that you felt compelled to state your own?

- You felt the other person was being long-winded, and you were too impatient to allow her to finish?

None of these are valid reasons to interrupt. Whatever you gain by getting your two cents in prematurely, you lose from a relationship perspective. You may be making a point of high value and impact, but the odds are your relationship partner will not respect or appreciate your ideas if he or she is interrupted by you. Again, "People don't care how much you know until they know how much you care."

The Sentence Finisher

This may seem like harmless enough behavior, but never forget this truth: "Others do not begin sentences for you to finish them." Because communication is what I do for a living, it took me until five or six years ago to figure this one out. Dale Carnegie hit the mark when he said, "We all love to hear the sound of our own voice." But when you finish people's sentences, what they are hearing is: "I know how to complete your thoughts better than you do." Most people who commit this sin do so with good intent. You think you're showing your colleagues that you're on the same wavelength, that you think alike. Or you're demonstrating to a client that you will not only meet his needs but also anticipate them.

Even if you can accurately anticipate what others have to say, they do not appreciate being spoken over or cut off in midsentence. In fact, finishing someone else's sentence is more off-putting than interrupting. It's one thing to stop someone from speaking. It's something else to speak for him.

If you have the tendency to jump in and complete people's sentences, next time you do it, watch the other person carefully. He may not say anything; but see if his eyes or body language reveal his true feelings. Do you see a slight grimace? Does he narrow his eyes or glare? Once you witness a negative reaction, you're less likely to make the same mistake. Most of the time, you will hear nothing directly, and he may show you nothing, but people like to start and finish their own sentences. Your negative behavior can impact a working relationship dramatically.

The Friendly Faker

If you are distracted by something around you or if something else going on in your life is preoccupying you, your attention may wander during conversations. Rather than admit you didn't absorb everything, you attempt to fake it. You nod your head. When the other person asks if you agree with him, you say yes. You remember one thing your relationship partner said and focus on that issue to demonstrate you were paying attention.

You may think you convinced the person you are speaking to that you are completely there, but you are probably wrong. Most people don't like drawing attention to the fact that the person they are speaking to is not listening. But, while they may not call you on it, they are aware that your mind was somewhere else. When you are fully listening and engaged, people feel it. You have probably experienced the reverse situation yourself. Perhaps while talking to a business colleague or a friend, you could *feel* he wasn't fully engaged. He may have been nodding and looking right at you, but you could sense he was distracted.

Remind yourself that other people can sense if you're not listening, so don't fake it. If you missed out on part of the conversation, force yourself to be honest and admit you didn't catch everything that was said. Request that the speaker repeat the specific portions that you did not fully hear. Apologize and ask for clarification or elaboration.

In this way, you're being honest rather than deceitful, since deceit can swiftly destroy trust—the hallmark of results-producing relationships.

The Rehearser

We are all guilty of rehearsing our agendas due to the excitement of contributing our thoughts and opinions. It's natural to think about how you're going to phrase a request for a raise or a bid for a new higher-profile assignment while the other person is talking. However, if you want the interaction to be win-win, rehearsing is a bad habit that must be broken. People can see it and sniff it out from a mile away.

Ideally, you'll do your rehearsing before your meeting. Of course, you have to think about what you're going to say in response to what she is telling you. This problem comes into play when you concentrate so much on what you're going to request or propose that you disconnect from the conversation.

The best way to avoid this disconnection is by rehearsing prior to the performance. Know what you're going to say before your meeting. Anticipate any objections your colleague may have. In this way, you'll free yourself from having to figure out what you're going to say on the fly. The easier you make it to concentrate on the other person, the more likely you'll be perceived as a good listener. If you have a good idea that you can't forget, try to think of one word that will trigger the thought so that you can resume listening but chime in intelligently after you've actively listened to them finish.

PRACTICING SILENCE AND OTHER LISTENING BEHAVIORS THAT WORK

Listening is far from a passive activity. If you are a passive hearer, you may take in some words but give nothing back. Listening requires concentration, effort, and a thoughtful response. It means you must work at listening with your head and heart and not just your ears. And it means learning how to respond to what is being said so that your listening communicates what your relationship partner needs to hear.

---

*It is the province of knowledge to speak, and
it is the privilege of wisdom to listen.*
—*Oliver Wendell Holmes*

There are seven steps you can take to gain listening wisdom:

1. *Practice silence.*

As the sins of the previous section suggested, remaining quiet can be a challenge. You're going to feel compelled to interrupt, to finish sentences, and to add your own ideas. It takes discipline to remain silent. Make a conscious effort to say nothing until you are sure your relationship partner has finished his thought. This is easier written than done. Therefore, try practicing it at home before you do it at work. With a spouse or a friend, force yourself to stay silent during a conversation until he is finished speaking. In many ways, it is more difficult to do this with someone you know well because conversations are often filled with frequent interruptions from both parties. By practicing silence in a personal relationship, though, you learn the discipline of knowing when to be silent in a professional encounter.

2. *Eliminate distractions.*

Corporate leaders are consistently criticized for their poor listening skills. This is because they *think* they are multitasking by staying busy while others are trying to seek their attention. However, what those managers don't realize is that they are contributing to the erosion of crucial relationships by allowing distractions. Shut the door, turn off your cell phone, and don't glance at the computer for e-mail. If appropriate—if your relationship partner has communicated that he feels this meeting is important—clear your schedule and tell him that he has all the time he needs to make his points. Similarly, during this meeting, don't bring up tangential or unrelated topics. You want the other person to feel you have done everything you can to make 100 percent listening you can. Many managers say, "My boss doesn't have time." My response is, "Leaders who want the best results make time."

3. *Focus your attention.*

This means you can't daydream, dwell on how you are going to respond, or tune out the other person. Giving your boss or customer your undivided attention is just that—a gift. Reflect on what she's trying to tell you—consider the literal meaning and read between the lines. Don't allow a ringing phone, a conversation going on outside the office, or anything else to distract you. People are remarkably sensitive to another individual's attention—or lack thereof. They can somehow tell if you're only listening at 50 percent. Give them 100 percent if you value the relationship and the results it can produce.

4. *Show nonverbal attentiveness.*

We communicate most of our messages without opening our mouths. It's not enough just to listen attentively; you need to demonstrate this attentiveness. Four easy ways to do this are: face the person directly, nod, make eye contact, and smile. Shifting uneasily in your seat or glancing around as if you're waiting for the police to arrest you are not ways to communicate your attentiveness. Impassive, immobile listeners seem bored. Use your eyes and body language to convey that you're anything but bored. Also, learn from the violators and think how much respect you lose for those who are nonverbally dismissive when you speak. Are they the people you want to work hard and get results for? Unlikely.

5. *Use the "repeat principle."*

Paraphrase what you thought the other person said. For instance, "If I'm hearing correctly, you're telling me that . . ." There are two immediate benefits to the repeat principle: (1) *You gain respect through giving it.* By asking them to repeat what you believe they communicated or intended is a great relationship connection to make, which leads to (2) *You clarify accuracy and eliminate misunderstandings.* Other business benefits include crisper, faster decision making and the prevention and mitigation of workplace errors.

You can't overuse this technique. If you do, you risk coming off as inattentive or hard of hearing. Wait until you need an explanation about what he's saying. Or wait until the other person says something with a lot of emphasis— either through his tone of voice or because he tells you, "This is important." This gives you the opportunity that you need to apply the repeat principle.

6. *Demonstrate empathy.*

While experiencing what other people are experiencing certainly helps us relate to others, it is not empathy. The traits that reflect a demonstration of empathy include compassion, shifts in perspective, and seeking to understand the other person's vantage point. It's one of the hallmarks of emotional intelligence, yet it is difficult to put our arms around because we don't feel the same way the other person feels, even if we share a common experience. Yet, when I ask participants in seminars to identify three great leaders, one of the most common responses is, "They really listened to me and tried to understand where I was coming from." The challenge with empathy is that it's not a stand-alone behavior, it's a mindset that doesn't include our own selfish motives; it's counter to how people act and what they're driven by. But I will boldly tell you that empathy builds strong emotional connections that expedite trust, loyalty, performance, and profit. Logic makes people think; emotional connections make people want to take action. Empathy is a direct pipeline; it's one of those breakthrough qualities that garners results, in and out of the workplace. Keep the wisdom of St. Francis of Assisi in your mind:

Seek first to understand, then to be understood.

7. Ask great questions.

Have you ever been in an audience when the speaker asks, "Does anyone have any questions?" and no one responds? It is as if she never spoke at all—or no one paid any attention to what she said. If you don't ask any questions during a conversation—or if you just ask perfunctory questions—you create the same effect. So don't be shy about asking a few good questions. Even one good question may be enough to show that you have been listening intently. If you've ever listened to a press conference, you know what I mean. Typically, a politician or pro sports coach is asked a bunch of inane questions, and then one member of the media asks the question that really sheds light on the situation. You want to be the one to ask that good question. Maybe your boss has just told you that she can't stand her own boss and doesn't know how to deal with his unreasonable requests, that she can't sleep nights, that she's spending too much work time trying to placate her boss instead of getting real work done. So your good question might be: "Can you talk to the CEO or someone in management and ask them to intervene?" or "Is there any way I can help you?" A good question demonstrates you've followed the logic of the conversation and are thinking about possible solutions/actions. That's the mark of a perceptive listener.

LISTEN WITH THE SELFLESS ATTITUDE OF A SAINT

Continuing with this theme, the superior listener must temporarily forsake his or her ego. To reap the full relationship benefits of being an exceptional listener, you must forget about *you*. Obviously, you do have an ego and you cannot disappear entirely—nor should you. But being able to do so at key times in a conversation will increase your value to the other person.

My cousin Chris is a brilliant listener. People who meet him are struck by what a great person he is, and they always ask me about Chris and express interest in getting together with him again soon. His secret is that he listens selflessly. That means he:

- Asks questions about *you.*
- Finds out what is bothering *you.*
- Discovers what *you* like.
- Responds with beneficial information for *you* based on what *you've* told him.

Chris exudes a charisma without talking about himself. He makes you the hero. He is so focused on other people that people find him a delightful conversation partner. In addition, the intensity of his focus on the people he meets allows him to remember details about them that most people would quickly forget. He can recall everything from where someone went to college to their favorite restaurant with uncanny accuracy. No doubt, this is due in part to Chris's inherently great memory. But it is also because he clearly communicates he is more concerned about what the other person has to say than stating his own opinions.

Results-producing relationships are 50–50 propositions. But in business situations, you gain a relationship and competitive advantage by initiating the listening process. As Dale Carnegie said:

> *You can make more friends in two months by becoming interested in other people than you can in two years of trying to get other people interested in you.*

One of the greatest benefits of being a good listener is that the more you listen selflessly, the more your relationship partner will also want to listen selflessly. Assuming this person isn't completely self-centered, he will likely reach a point in the conversation where he realizes he's doing all the talking and you're doing all the listening. Recognizing that he has been monopolizing the conversation, he will likely turn the focus to you. He'll also feel grateful that you've allowed him to have his say and that you've done such a good job of absorbing his words. As a result, the balance in conversational exchanges will tilt back to the 50-50 ideal.

ARE YOU LISTENING? A SELF-AUDIT

Do you consider yourself a good listener? Most people respond affirmatively to this question. They think about how they listened patiently to their boss complain for what seemed like hours about a new organizational policy or remained attentive when a customer did spend hours going over complaints about service.

But endurance isn't the same as listening. Remaining silent and trying to pay attention doesn't mean you are being a good listener. It takes a conscious, more concentrated effort. To determine if you are making this effort, answer the questions that follow. When responding, recall a recent meeting with an influential person in your company or a customer or client who has a significant impact on your work life. Consider these questions in light of that recent meeting:

- Were you attentive throughout the conversation; did you make sure you didn't drift off, daydream, or lose the thread of the discussion at any point?

- Did you let him complete his thought; did you consciously stop yourself from interrupting?

- Did you listen with your entire body; did you make an effort to maintain eye contact, to nod when you agreed, to smile when you thought something was funny?

- If the other person expressed a strong feeling about the subject being discussed, did you communicate your empathy in some way—through your verbal response, the look in your eyes, or gestures?

- Every so often, did you restate what your relationship partner said?

- If you did miss something during the conversation or weren't clear about it, did you request clarification?

- Did you do everything possible to eliminate distractions during the talk; did you turn off your cell, avoid checking e-mail messages, and tune out conversations going on in the hallway outside the office?

- Did you demonstrate verbally that you absorbed what was being communicated; did you make comments or ask questions that demonstrated you *got it*?

How many yes answers did you have? While you may not have been able put a yes next to all the questions, it's a good litmus test to illustrate the complexities of complete listening. You'll find it's also a good contrast-and-compare list to complete with spouses at home or team members at work. No one is perfect, and there are going to be times when you don't make eye contact or when you get distracted. The key to becoming a better listener is to become aware of these moments in real time.

Now try this exercise in another situation. Wait until your boss or customer calls you and asks to sit down to discuss an important topic. Review these eight questions before the meeting. Then, after the meeting, review your responses. The odds are that you will have more yes responses than before. Just being conscious of the questions will encourage you to exhibit good listening skills.

Awareness of your listening weaknesses is also crucial. Everyone has at least some weak spots when it comes to listening, and they are generally related to one or more of these eight questions. But in practice, the weakness can take a number of specific behavioral forms. The following is a list of statements of listening weakness. Review them and determine which one or ones apply to you:

- I interrupt people constantly. I know I shouldn't, but when they say something I know is wrong, I can't help myself.

- I can't stand it when people give speeches instead of just talking; I lose all focus when this happens.

- I think I must have some sort of attention-deficit disorder when it comes to listening to authority figures— a spider crawling across a conference room table can distract me.

- I get bored easily, and if the person I'm talking to isn't saying something interesting, I just nod my head and fake like I'm listening.

- I rarely ask questions after a conversation with a boss or a client; I'm worried that they'll think I'm stupid for asking the obvious.

- I'm good at paying attention when a discussion is about me, but when it's about things that only concern the other person, then I lose my concentration.

- I listen closely, but then my mind shifts to what I want to say in response, and I don't hear everything that's being said.

If none of these statements describes your particular listening weakness, create one that does. Write it out and keep that piece of paper handy—the more you remind yourself of the weakness, the better you'll be at managing it.

THE FOXHOLE PRINCIPLE: WHY YOU CAN DEPEND ON THE BEST LISTENERS

After my mother and father celebrated their 40th wedding anniversary, I asked them who their three closest friends were. They named three people, and then I asked them to name the three best listeners they had ever met. No surprise: They named their three closest friends.

This is not unusual. The people we feel closest to, whether personally or professionally, are usually great listeners. We may have friends and colleagues we enjoy being around for their insight, their entertainment value, and their power/influence, but the ability to listen trumps all other factors. When things get tough, we want people who can listen to be in the foxhole with us. When we are scared or dealing with big challenges, we want someone to whom we can express what's going through our minds.

CEOs and other top managers often have wonderful resources available to them, but even so, they are often bad at listening. Because of their positions, leaders can talk and expect that their audience will be attentive. Yet, as I noted earlier, people know when they're really being listened to versus being heard. They sense when the attention is perfunctory; when people are listening politely but not passionately, and they truly appreciate those who listen deeply and responsively.

You can be one of those people. If you can master the art of listening, you will be invaluable to a person of influence. Think about someone you know who really listens to you. How do you feel about that individual? I would bet that you feel trusting, grateful, and empowered. When someone feels similarly about you in a professional relationship, you're the one he's likely to turn to when he needs help. And ultimately, this quiet skill will have more of an impact on your career than articulating 100 great ideas frequently and loudly.

Simplify and Apply

Two years ago, I worked with an executive named John, and he was stunned at the shellacking assessment about his leadership from this employees. Every person said, "Very poor listener." I learned quickly that John was a high-energy guy with good intent, but poor impact.

In digging deep and learning specifically where he was "very poor" in his listening, we discovered it was in the distractions department. John would actually call people into his office and make more eye contact with his computer than with the person he called in. His behavior focus: Face the person and totally focus on their words and clarify their needs and how you can help.

Three months later, John's follow-up assessment was like his mother wrote it. Comments included, "Different person, highly improved. Shows he cares about people more than process." My favorite of all: "Four months ago, I had my resume ready to go to work for anyone but John. Today, I would not work for anyone but John."

Sometimes, the little nuggets you extract from these awareness points serve as triggers that can make a difference. Look for those as you read on.

CHAPTER SEVEN

Get to Know the Complete Person

Do you know that your boss intends to move to the country and open a bed-and-breakfast when he retires in ten years? Are you aware that your customer is a serious student of Yoga and meditates every evening?

It is frighteningly common how much we don't know about personal passions and the things that really make people tick, yet we spend more hours with many of them than with our own families. We also don't know much about our coworkers' career hopes and dreams or their failures and frustrations. Often, we only know the bare minimum necessary to work together effectively. Sure we might chit-chat about nonwork activities—a professional football game, a movie, a child's accomplishment. But we consider this nonessential information. It doesn't contribute to making us or them more productive or effective at work.

Or does it? The reality is that if you keep your relationships on strictly professional footing, you limit their potential. If there isn't a mutual exchange not only of personal information but feelings about things personal and professional,

113

you can limit the results the relationship produces. A bond of trust and understanding will be missing from the relationship—a bond that motivates people to do more for relationship partners than they would do for anyone else.

Getting to know the complete person is not something you can achieve in one meeting or one week. You don't want to be a creepy stalker and say, "Janice, we've been working together for three years, and it's time for you to tell me everything I need to know about who you are," and have colleagues run for cover. This is especially true if you have had a purely professional relationship for months or years, and now are looking to take the relationship to the next level. Patience and persistence are called for in these instances. You must be natural and incremental about your inquiries. Additionally, you can't demand information or ask questions that make you sound like you are prying. With these caveats in mind, consider what details you need to learn about your relationship partners . . . and why it's important to learn a wide range of things.

IT'S NOT ENOUGH TO KNOW THE NAMES OF YOUR BOSS'S KIDS AND HIS GOLF HANDICAP

When I tell people they need to know the complete person, they tell me that they know their customers' favorite restaurants, the names and ages of their kids, and the kind of coffee they order from Starbucks. All of this is fine to know, but it is only a start. To understand the complete person, delve deeper and explore wider.

Be aware, too, that you really need to express your interest in getting to know that other person. If you don't like him or don't really care about establishing a fuller relationship, you are not going to succeed. By that I mean that other people are usually more perceptive than you give them credit for. Consciously or not, they recognize a pattern of interactions that signifies real interest, and a pattern that signifies self-interest. Your tone of voice, your memory of how they responded to a question you asked the previous week, your response when they tell you something confidential—all of it communicates whether you are sincere or feigning interest.

While you can't be expected to like everyone, if you aren't curious about your relationship partners, then you need to look for other partners. Results-producing relationships don't happen when you are unaware of the quirks, long-term goals, and hobbies of your relationship partners. Throw away all your false assumptions about what a good working relationship should be—impersonal, filled with information boundaries, purely pragmatic—and replace them with some new relationship realities.

The biggest new reality? You're forging an emotional connection in a relationship that has always been purely logical. Most business relationships tend to be one-dimensional and connected by logic: You supply needed services, and your customer pays for those services; you adapt what you do when your customer requests some changes. This is fine, but consider the following truism that I learned from consulting guru, Alan Weiss.

Logic makes people think, emotion makes them act.

Emotions often prompt us to make significant, new purchases. Logic may make us interested in making the purchase, but it is emotion that is the catalyst. We reason that we need a new SUV because we are going to be driving a lot in the snowbelt, but it is only when we get in the SUV, take it for a test-drive, and feel good about the experience that we are compelled to buy. In the same way, emotion acts as a catalyst for your relationship partners to take action on your behalf. Relationship partners are much more likely to put in a good word for you with their bosses or to provide you with additional resources if you have forged emotional connections. And when you get to know the complete person, you help forge that connection.

THE COMPLETE PERSON QUESTIONNAIRE

The following questionnaire is designed as a guide to the type of information you should seek from your relationship partners. You may want to skip some of the questions and substitute ones that work better for you. It is more important to get a sense of the range of information these questions represent. As you can see, they start with simple, factual inquiries and proceed to questions about intangibles—hopes, fears, and so on. Following each question is an explanation of how a given piece of information can help you know the complete person as well as a tip about how to obtain the information.

1. *Where were you raised?*
You may know where your business colleagues live now, but it is quite possible that you are unaware of where they grew up. This is relevant information in that it offers an opportunity for an emotional connection. People have strong feelings—both pro and con—about hometowns, high schools, and so on. You may find that you had similar feelings about adolescence or that you know someone who grew up in the same place as your partner.

Tip

Participation in high school sports, similarities in family situations (i.e., child of divorce), and knowledge of a particular geographical area often lead to more meaningful interactions than the usual conversations about where someone is from.

---

2. *Where did you go to college?*
Again, college is an emotionally resonant experience. Everything from the name of the college football team, to whether

they participated in a fraternity or sorority, to their favorite subjects in school are good topics.

Tip
_____

Search for overlapping college experiences. Perhaps your two colleges were sports rivals or you had a good friend who went to the same school.

---

3. *What are your favorite movies/television shows/books/ musical artists?*

The odds are that your relationship partner will be passionate about at least one of these four topics. The discussion may start out about a specific program or piece of music, but this information can often reveal deeper aspects of an individual's formerly hidden personality. He might start out talking about a movie he loved that took place in Alaska, then segue into a trip he took to Alaska when he was younger, and then move on to how not staying in Alaska is one of his biggest regrets.

Tip
_____

Encourage the transitions from the specific event to the emotional response. In addition, pose thought-provoking questions to get the conversation started such as, "Which two musical performers, past or present, would you want to see perform live?"

---

4. *What are your hobbies or other passionate areas of interest (besides work)?*

People come alive when you tap into their passions. Even the most by-the-numbers business managers who are always on an even keel when dealing with work issues suddenly become animated when they talk about being an amateur chef or going on archaeological digs. These are subjects that bring out the real person who may be hiding behind a businesslike facade.

5. *What has been your biggest job challenge?*

Tip

If you really want to get to know someone, discover what she spends most of her spare time doing. Encourage people to open up about their hobbies or outside interests by talking about your own. Once you share that you collect antique beer mugs, they might reveal that they are also collectors. If you find yourself interested in their hobbies, learn more about them, and communicate to that person that you value those hobbies. If the hobbies truly interest you, arrange to go with your relationship partner to an event related to the hobby.

This question provides people with a way to share their insecurities, vulnerabilities, and frustrations. Your boss might start talking about how difficult it is to deal with his own boss. Your client may open up about his concern that he lacks the knowledge and resources to take his business global. These conversations allow you to see a side of your relationship partner that he may have kept hidden. Many times, people are hesitant to show a supplier or a direct report their soft side; they think they need to project an image of command and control. Their hesitation, however, can be overcome with the right question at the right time.

Tip

To make sure you ask the right question at the right time, watch for clues that your relationship partner wants to discuss a challenge she is facing. Again, you can't simply ask the question out of the blue. Wait until your boss says something like, "Sorry I've been so distracted, but I've been wrestling with a problem." In an indirect way, he is giving you permission to ask a question beyond the boundaries of your business relationship.

---

6. *Who are three of the most significant people in your life?*
Your relationship partners have lives outside of work,
though you may not know it. Do you know your boss's
spouse's name? Have you ever met her? Do you know if
your customer has children or if she has a best friend
in the same business? The answers may seem like they
are none of your business because they have nothing to
do with business, but that's not true. Creating artificial
boundaries separating personal and professional aspects
of your life is a practice of a bygone era. Limits on conversational topics place limits on the relationship. Therefore,
feel free to share this type of information with your partner
and see if she responds in kind.

Tip

Observe and respect resistance. It is important that you not
push someone to talk about his spouse or friend if he is clearly
uncomfortable. At the same time, be alert for repeated mentions
of an individual's name: "Paul and I went to the game yesterday"
or "This weekend, Jane made a great flourless chocolate cake."
These types of statements may not say much about these people, but by mentioning the names, they are issuing you an invitation to ask about them.

---

7. *What was your most embarrassing moment?*
Embarrassing moments reveal our human side. The
humor, as well as the pain, that emerges from these stories provide ways to connect that don't always arise when
discussing business. When we admit to doing something
dumb or silly, we admit that we're "just like you"—people
can identify with our embarrassment.

Again, this isn't a question you can just blurt out.
Many times, work situations present you with a natural
opening to talk about embarrassing moments. You may
be attending a presentation and the speaker inadvertently
says something inappropriate that draws a big laugh,

and the speaker turns red. You discuss this incident with your boss, and it becomes natural to share embarrassing events—both work-related and not.

Tip

Listen without judgment. By definition, embarrassing moments are sensitive subjects. You don't want to say, "Wow, that was really stupid; how could you have done that?" The whole point is to allow the other person to feel comfortable sharing this part of himself, so don't make fun or criticize.

These seven questions are not definitive ones. No doubt, you can come up with 101 other questions to ask that will provide you with specifically targeted insights about your relationship partners. So don't become hung up on these seven. As long as you find common ground in areas outside of the usual business discussion areas, you're on your way to knowing the complete person.

GETTING STARTED: THE TRICK OF ASKING A BOUNDARY-CROSSING QUESTION

You may have read the previous seven suggestions and thought they made sense. But putting them into action may feel awkward or challenging. This is especially true if you are dealing with an influential person with whom you've had only a marginal business relationship for months or years. If the boundaries of what is appropriate have been well-defined, to ask anything personal or career focused may seem like a violation of unwritten rules. If this is the case, you may be hesitant to appear too inquisitive.

Going beyond work-related details can be awkward initially. It is important to be aware that contrary to what you might fear, your relationship partners are probably eager to share with you their concerns about their careers or news about their children. As Benjamin Disraeli once noted, "Talk to a man about himself, and he'll listen for hours." No matter how important or powerful people are, they usually share a need to communicate their hopes and fears, their daily personal dramas, and their excitement about a local sports team or a recent concert.

Getting started is a matter of willpower; it also requires finding some easy entry points for discussion. Here are some suggestions:

- *Google the names of your relationship partners.* In many cases, you will learn details about them that you didn't know before. I remember once being in a meeting with a client's CEO. Prior to the meeting, I had googled his name and discovered that he sat on the board of a ballet company. When I mentioned this fact in passing during the meeting, his eyes lit up. Here are some common bits of information you are likely to learn through a Google search: college attended; any publications or speeches; memberships on boards, voluntary committees, community organizations; participation in amateur sports events (i.e., marathons). All of this provides you with useful conversation topics. You don't need to tell the other person you were googling him. You can simply use the information to start a discussion. For instance, "You know, I was thinking about running the Chicago Marathon. Do you know anyone who has run it?"

- *Tell a story.* This is an indirect way of moving beyond established conversational boundaries. Instead of asking what feels like an intrusive question, you tell a story that invites the other person to respond with a related story—one that reveals more about her than she ordinarily would. Perhaps someone in your organization is fired, and you talk about how you got fired from a summer job in high school because you overslept and showed up late one day. This is an invitation to your relationship partner to tell her own getting-fired story. We get to know people better by hearing their stories, and you should not be shy of introducing stories into your relationships.

- *Ask simple, natural questions.* Don't labor to ask brilliant, insightful, long-winded questions. People reveal details about themselves in response to what seems like innocuous inquiries. One of the best is, "Did you do anything fun last weekend?" or "Do you have any plans for this weekend?" Choose a time to ask these questions that feels natural. You should give the other person a chance to discuss an aspect of his personal life in a nonthreatening way. Over time, you can be a bit more ambitious in the questions you ask, for example, "What's your favorite part of your job?" Or "If you could do anything else but this, what would it be?" The key is to ask these questions simply and naturally. If they feel awkward or forced, that's okay, you are practicing a new behavior. But the more you ask, the more you'll see how much people like talking about themselves. In time, a natural confidence will emerge as a logical part of the conversation, the questions you ask, and the connections you make.

ARE YOU READY FOR COMPLETE RELATIONSHIPS?

Not everyone is. You may be the sort of person who is shy, lacks self-confidence, or gives up after one rejection to a boundary-defying question. When people fail to get to know their bosses, direct reports, or customers fully, it's often a result of internal rather than external factors. It may seem like your boss is giving you the brush-off when you try to explore some deeper topics with him; or your direct reports or customers may think you have a hidden agenda, but I've learned through practice that it all begins with internal dialogue.

While some awkwardness is natural, and most people experience some discomfort as they try to get to know the complete person, it is important to overcome those feelings. To do so, you must first be aware of what might be holding you back. To help create that awareness, consider the following questions:

• *Do you engage in positive self-talk?*
We've all heard it, but when the dialogue taking place in your head is supportive, it gives you a base to take chances. You're self-aware and confident, you don't start questioning every move you make. You give yourself the strength necessary to take people risks. You don't become discouraged if those risks don't pay off immediately. Positive self-talk offers you a way to analyze conversations with a boss or customer in ways that foster learning. If you ask about your boss's children and you don't get much of a response, you are able to self-talk your way through the problem. You may discover that you need to ask different questions to get a more satisfying response.

• *Are you courageous?*
You need to be willing to take the risk of getting to know the complete person. This means asking questions that you may not have asked in the past. It also means being willing to answer similar questions yourself. You possess the courage, but you need to motivate yourself to act on that courage—that's what *being* courageous is all about. Do you want to have a richer, more productive relationship with an influential person? Then you're going to have to take a chance and get to know them . . . and let them get to know you. Deeper connections open bigger opportunities.

• *Do you possess a genuine interest in other people?*
Do you consider yourself a person who is interested in others? Do you relish meeting new people? Do you naturally try to figure out their stories? Are you fascinated by who people really are and want to discover how they got that way? If so, you're in a good position to get to know the complete person. If you're not, no worries. The steps in these chapters are no different from any skill you acquire; the more you practice the behavior, the faster that behavior turns into habit.

The Introverts Turn Around

I cannot cite the source, but I remember reading about a study group of 33 self-described introverts who were paid to "act extroverted" and get to know the personal interests of others at a networking function. They were given specific questions to ask and trained how to respond and dig deeper. In the postgroup interview, 29 out of 33 said they liked how people responded to them and would employ some of their more confident behaviors. The results they received were worth the investment even though it was initially uncomfortable for them.

• *Are you able to manage your ego?*
If you're overly wrapped up in your own issues, you may lack the motivation and energy to find out about other people. People with the capacity for selflessness can push their own issues to the side and focus on others. Having this ability helps enormously if you want to know about more than just superficial aspects of other people.

• *Are you persistent?*
Getting to know someone fully sometimes requires a little stubbornness. Your relationship partners may rebuff your initial efforts to get them to talk about themselves. Or they

may respond but not show much enthusiasm for the subject. That means you may have to keep at it. You might have to ask the same question in a different way or in a different setting. It's surprising how people who are resistant to talk about personal issues in the office are much more willing to do so on a plane or while eating a meal or having a drink. Persistence gives you second, third, and fourth chances to get others to open up.

• *Do you ask interesting, open-ended questions?*
Some people have the knack of posing questions that make others want to talk about themselves. This is much more effective than asking questions that have yes or no answers. Think about it this way. Let's say you want to know where your customer goes for three weeks every summer—you know he takes a big block of time off every August. You could ask, "Do you take golf vacations every August?" Or you could ask: "I've always imagined that when you take those three-week vacations in August, you do something incredibly exciting like exploring some third world country or going on some wilderness adventure. Maybe you're just golfing, but I would bet it's more than that, right?"

• *After you ask your questions, are you focused and fully engaged?*
You may ask about whether your relationship partner enjoys volunteering at the local soup kitchen, but if you don't seem intent on hearing the answer, you won't receive much of an answer. You must listen to answers with your whole being. You want people to have the impression that you are eager to hear their answers. If you're a focused and fully engaged listener, you will encourage people to share aspects of their lives that they normally don't discuss at work. People are more likely to share when they sense the other person cares.

IT'S QUALITY, NOT QUANTITY

Business associates do not have to be your best friends. You don't have to spend hours each day examining aspects of their character. You are not their therapist, nor should you be. There are certain things that are truly personal, and neither you nor your relationship partner should share them with anyone except a family member or best friend.

I've learned that you can get to know the complete person a lot faster than you might expect. As I emphasized earlier, it is not going to happen overnight. But in a few months time, you should be well on your way to developing a fuller sense of who your relationship partner is. Sometimes, a few questions (like the ones mentioned in this chapter) can create the common ground that was never established with years of business-only connections. Positive results are natural and inevitable when you invest in discovering the complete person. If you both are willing to share more of who you are—from your love of baseball to your concern about a sibling's lack of a job—you are going to create a stronger bond, and the relationship will produce more results.

It just stands to reason. Think about the people you know best in the world and who know you best. How much have they done for you? How much would they be willing to do for you? When you make the effort to know someone completely, you naturally become closer and more willing to help each other.

So, make the effort and discover how the relationship can become more productive than it ever was in the past. But capture that information in writing so you can reference it going forward. Building a database allows you to transition from learning *who people are* to the more success-yielding connection of learning *what they are about.*

CHAPTER EIGHT

Tell Yourself the Truth (and Get Others to Help You)

Going to a new level of success requires your willingness to solicit honest feedback and your ego's willingness to accept it.

While ego can drive job performance and career achievement, it can also stand in the way of self-honesty and effectiveness. If your ego goes unmanaged—if you allow it to dictate your thoughts and actions—then you are at risk of filtering out any negative feedback and only hearing the positive. Throughout this chapter, you will see how easy it is for all of us to practice self-deception. While it can manifest itself in myriad ways, the primary culprit behind self-deceptive behavior is usually an unmanaged ego.

People whose egos shield them from the truth of their shortcomings are incapable of forging deeper work relationships. Not only are they incapable of taking these relationships to higher, more productive levels, they may also lack the capacity to sustain them at all. The following example illustrates the profound impact "ego blindness" can have on relationships.

As senior manager in an industry-leading company, John was a talented, knowledgeable executive whose management style reflected his background as a high school football star. Like the most stereotypical of bullying coaches, John believed in management through intimidation. For this reason, it wasn't unusual for him to express his displeasure by yelling at direct reports. Even worse, at times, he would lose his temper in client meetings. Insecure and wanting to control every situation he was in, John was very difficult to work with.

Contrary to his bullying demeanor, John was also a considerate man with a kind heart, and there were instances where he would display these qualities by going beyond the call of duty to help direct reports and colleagues. In John's own mind, he was tough but fair. He had convinced himself that his rigid and demanding style made him a highly valuable and effective manager; he saw the positive aspects of being tough but none of the negative ones. Even when his boss reprimanded him for his temper tantrums or micromanaging tendencies, John rationalized these negative comments, telling himself that his boss didn't realize how it was sometimes necessary to seize control of a situation or let someone know that if she made a mistake, it wouldn't be tolerated a second time. His ego, in short, blinded him to his own faults.

For five years, John's boss supported him despite concerns expressed by the CEO and other top executives that John's style might not be right for their firm. He valued John's contributions because bosses love those who get things done, and he falsely assumed that with time and experience, John would change. Unfortunately, too many things came undone with John. His intimidating manner became more oppressive despite his boss's requests that he "tone it down." After one particularly unpleasant exchange between John and the firm's largest client, John's boss admitted there was a problem and bowed to pressure from his bosses to let John go.

This is a sobering story to begin the chapter with, but a necessary one to serve up because too many people exhibit behaviors that contradict goodness but refuse to acknowledge the truth from themselves or others. It's not always easy to admit faults or insecurities to others, and it's often even more challenging to admit them to yourself. Yet when you're not brutally honest about your own short-comings, you risk losing trust and credibility from others. This deadly combination can wield a devastating blow to both to your reputation and business relationships as evidenced by John's professional demise.

Now, we are going to explore insights that explain why we don't hear or even probe for the truth so that we are cognizant of the pitfalls and recognize opportunities to move forward. And, as will be the case with all chapters, you will find behavioral techniques that work for getting results, truthful results.

It is not unusual to practice some self-deception because your ego is on the line when you are looking in the mirror. Recognize, though, that this self-deception can permit you to make a statement about yourself, but that statement is contradicted when others know the opposite is true. You may insist that you want to take on a big, time-consuming project at work, but the truth is that you lack the time, discipline, and experience to handle it.

None of this is intended to prescribe negative self-talk, but rather, to encourage realistic optimism. Character and integrity are integral baseline foundations from which we are assessed by colleagues and customers. Influencing others to contribute to success begins when you discover the truth about yourself. To help you learn to be truthful with yourself, let's look at the most common ways people deceive themselves. Keep your self-assessment hat on as you read through the next section.

TYPES OF SELF-DECEPTION

People tend to hide the truth from about themselves in many ways. It may be a small way, such as telling ourselves that we weren't rude on the phone to a vendor soliciting business when in fact we were abrupt and discourteous. It may be a more significant lie, such as denying to ourselves that we are in the wrong company or even the wrong field. It may be a one-time deception or it may continue for weeks, months or in too many sad cases, for years.

So there's no end to the ways we can lead ourselves astray. Here is a list of the five most common self-deception tactics:

1. Refusing to acknowledge problems or weaknesses.
2. Playing the victim.
3. Believing that if you didn't have bad luck, you'd have no luck at all.
4. Convincing yourself that you lack what it takes.
5. Overinflating your capacities.

Refusing to Acknowledge Problems or Weaknesses

If you're unable to admit to yourself that you lack certain knowledge or skills or that you've come up short on an assignment, you will be unable to recognize your need for improvement in this area. If you've been a high-performance person from the time you started school, this is an especially tough admission. It seems better to fool yourself into believing you're still an A student than accepting that you received a C-. You tell yourself a project failed because you weren't given enough time or other resources. You're convinced that you don't need additional training to move to the next performance level, even though more than one person has advised you that's exactly what you do need.

If you deny that you're having problems, you're never going to improve your performance in the eyes of others. Business associates may assume that you are stuck at your current level and that you are unable or unwilling to progress beyond it.

It is frustrating for consultants and corporate leaders alike to work with people who refuse to look inward. I once coached a brilliantly intellectual bank president named Jane. She had a great education and business background; she was passionate about her job and helping customers. However, an assessment from her employees revealed a consistent pattern—Jane was closed-minded in high pressure situations. When I confronted Jane with this feedback, she snapped, "That's simply not true. I have to make executive decisions," to which I responded, "But your employees are confused about why you ask their opinions but never implement their ideas. That seems to be why they feel this way."

Still flustered and hurt, Jane became firmer, "Well, I'm not closed-minded!"

For me, Jane's situation is, in a professional sense, tragic. She has so much natural drive and intelligence to succeed, but she prevents herself from going to that next level of performance. The utter irony was that almost every direct report on her executive board said she was closed-mind, yet she responded with a closed mind . . . about being closed-minded.

Consultant Alan Weiss says, "You cannot empower those unwilling to be empowered."

People who are unwilling to be enlightened by others display the most obvious symptoms of self-deception.

Playing the Victim

You tell yourself that it's not your fault that you have been victimized by people or circumstances beyond your control, and rather than accept responsibility for your actions, you create fictitious scapegoats. "If my customer wasn't such a tightwad, I would have the resources to achieve the goals he sets" or "I'm never going to shine unless my boss gives me the freedom to do things my way instead of his way" are just a couple of typical examples of playing the victim. There is no doubt that there are many times when colleagues or customers don't provide you with sufficient resources or freedom, but when you use that as an excuse and make it into a bigger obstacle than it really is, then you're guilty of self-deception.

And what you tell yourself has the propensity to be acted out in subsequent behaviors. You probably won't accuse your boss or client of victimizing you, but you may fall prey to doing or saying things that inadvertently convey this impression. You convey negative resistance about a reduced budget or act put out when people ask you to accomplish a task. You may not even be conscious of these behaviors, but your team members will be.

Believing If You Didn't Have Bad Luck, You'd Have No Luck at All

With apologies to Ray Charles who penned those lines, many people who quote them convince themselves that fate, the gods, or whoever controls luck is working against them. They convince themselves that some outside force is altering their job performance, personal effectiveness, and career success. Alternately, when they do well, they attribute it to the efforts of other people. It's almost as if they have reverse scapegoats—people to blame for their success.

People who deceive themselves in this way strike their colleagues as hesitant to take innovative chances and terrified of any risk. These individuals are always advising caution and warning of potential risks. They rarely make bold decisions and always seem like they're waiting for the other shoe to drop.

If this describes you, consider that playing not to lose damages the faith that others have in you, and can significantly impact reliability in your performance as a contributor and leader. It's important to make thoughtful, strategic decisions, but in every industry I've worked in, people do not like being around or working for people who constantly base decisions on worst-case scenarios. Similarly, most clients are unlikely to refer business to a service provider or businessperson who doesn't possess a can-do, solution-focused attitude.

Convincing Yourself You Lack What It Takes

If you tell yourself that you lack the experience or expertise to get the job done, it will ultimately affect your ability to do just that. Subconsciously convincing yourself that you aren't sufficiently assertive, innovative, or competent enough to handle an assignment will influence both your confidence at work and the impression others have of your abilities. Again, thoughts tend to dictate behaviors. If you make a strong enough impression, you may effectively convince others that you will never be able to live up to their expectations. As Vince Lombardi said, "Confidence is contagious, unfortunately, so is a lack of confidence."

What makes this worse is when we don't acknowledge that this negative self-talk is a bigger barrier than anyone outside ourselves. These inner arguments can become self-fulfilling prophecies. If you tell yourself you don't have what it takes, your perception becomes so convincing that you sabotage yourself. All your doubts and insecurities manifest themselves in your performance and demeanor. To those with whom you work, you come across as terribly insecure. As a result, both colleagues and customers are reluctant to entrust you with important assignments or business needs because your actions or attitude communicates that you can't handle it. The fastest way to rid yourself of negative self-talk is to first admit that it impedes your success and to then respond to that talk with assertive, confident behavior. I've coached both entry-level employees and high-level execs, and this application has worked wonders for breaking through to the next level. Get out of your own way!

Overinflating Your Capacities

While many people refuse to admit their own weaknesses, others hyperbolize their strengths. If you have a tendency to exaggerate your abilities, you tell yourself that you are the company's best salesperson, when in reality you are simply in the upper 50 percent. You may go so far as to insist to yourself that you have a good shot at the vice president opening, when the reality is that the probability is highly unlikely.

While being positive and optimistic is essential to achieving goals, your perception of your capabilities must be grounded in reality if they are to serve you well. You may convince yourself that the level of your abilities and your career trajectory are greater than they are, but you are not going to deceive your relationship partners. If you promise your customers the impossible and don't deliver, you are not going to have those customers for long, and not keeping your word can sustain and amplify a bad reputation.

Dramatizing your abilities is much different from imagining your potential. Creating statements like, "I'm not capable of managing that account right now, but I will be able to in a year with more experience under my belt," are important parts of assessing your performance and setting goals. It is important to be both ambitious and confident, but also realistic about whether you're ready for a project or position that could do more to help your career.

The lines can become blurred between positive self-talk and unrealistic capabilities based on a number of factors, including skill-base, knowledge, and experience. While it's challenging to maintain self-objectivity, hiding what we know to be true about our own abilities or potential for money, opportunity, or status can backfire.

My experience coaching business individuals and teams has provided me with a remarkably consistent insight into human behavior: we are terrified of admitting, to others and to ourselves, who we really are. I attribute this predominantly to the fear of failure. CEOs fear letting their employees down, so they tell themselves they must "always be confident." But confidence and vulnerability are not the same thing. Remember the story about Peter Davoren, CEO of Turner Construction? He won over a group of 100 employees with his statement, "I feel completely over my head. But where I quickly gain confidence is by knowing that I am surrounded by people like you to help all of us continue to succeed and grow as a team."

Davoren told himself and others the truth and look at the trust he gained, the way he got others to relate to him and to perform, which added exponentially to bottom-line profit. Turner Construction is not an industry leader by accident—it all started with their fearless leader who was not afraid to be vulnerable and truthful.

If we are so proficient at deceiving ourselves, how can we ever rectify the discrepancy between our perceptions and the truth about our abilities? The people with whom you have the closest relationship in work environments can generally see through these lies. They know you better than anyone—sometimes better than you know yourself.

RESULTS YOU DON'T WANT

People generally think, "What happens inside me stays inside me." Despite my earlier suggestions that being dishonest with yourself will dramatically impact the interaction you have with your colleagues and customers, you may doubt that the impact is significant enough to warrant change. After all, it is not as if you are bragging to your boss that you can do anything, or that you told your customers how doubtful you were that you could handle his most important request.

But the truth is that people are more perceptive and can see right through you, your overconfidence, or your excuses. You hold a lot of what you know about others inside, but you never communicate it. Over time, people pick up on the evidence you inadvertently leave behind. It can be anything from an uncertain tone to an unwillingness to work on a particular team to dominating a staff meeting. Behaviors that suggest insecurity, uncertainty, inconsistency, or a reluctance to take ownership for your actions can elicit the following results:

- *A perception that you are not trustworthy:* When you hide from yourself or seem as if you are lacking self-awareness, you may give others the impression that you are sneaky, dishonest, or at the very least not forthcoming. Maybe you don't make eye contact during conversations, or perhaps you give the impression that you are holding information back. No matter what your behavior, if you are being dishonest with yourself, it could be interpreted by others as untrustworthiness.

- *Poor connections:* Unless you are completely honest with yourself, you cannot form deep relationships with others. If you reveal only select parts of who you really are, you may trigger reservations

or skepticism from those with whom you are looking to develop partnering relationships. Ultimately,
you may never be able to forge the close emotional
bonds that elevate relationships to results-producing
levels.

- *A lack of leadership ability:* People who cannot accept
  their shortcomings or are unconscious of them actually repel others. The best leaders are in touch with
  who they are at their core and conscious of how who
  they are affects others. Their confidence, competence,
  and charisma all emanate from the commitment of
  being transparent—with themselves as well as with
  others. When you meet these people, it is immediately apparent that what you see is what you get.
  You are drawn to them instinctively. When you practice self-deception, you deny yourself the opportunity
  to be a real leader. Your boss will not be able to see
  past your dishonesty or poor self-assessment to view
  you as leadership material, and even if he does,
  direct reports won't want to follow you.

In work situations, people often become so consumed
by daily tasks that they overlook the effect their internal
dishonesty is having on how others perceive them until
significant damage has been done. Molly, a young partner at a large computer consulting firm was facing this
exact situation when I was hired by the firm to help them
improve internal relations. Having been named partner at
a relatively young age because of her analytical brilliance,
Molly developed a sense of superiority. Because she was
given a lot of responsibility and was able to handle it well,
she developed an overinflated sense of self-worth. The
internal dialogues that helped her accurately assess her
performance and question her actions stopped. She began
disregarding that little voice in her head that suggested

there might be better ways of handling given situations, and instead, convinced herself she could do no wrong.

Of course, she did do wrong. In her early years in the firm, she developed a strong relationship with a major client. Because she proved herself reliable and trustworthy, this client trusted her opinions and followed her direction implicitly. After Molly became partner, stopped being true to herself, and lost sight of her responsibilities, she made a recommendation to the client that had a very negative outcome. Rather than apologizing to the client, Molly defended her recommendation and said the problem must have been the way the client implemented her recommended strategy. Everyone makes mistakes, even major ones, but honest self-talk is the first voice to listen to. Yet Molly refused to accept any responsibility or admit culpability, which resulted in a breakdown in the relationship between Molly and the important client—a break that resulted in the client (a twelve-year, high-paying client) giving the firm an ultimatum—pull Molly from the account or they would find business elsewhere. Molly's partners knew she was at fault and pulled her from the account. It was only after this significant event that she started to realize that she had been hiding from herself, that she was afraid of showing any self-doubt because it would ruin her idealized image of herself as the firm's superhero, and that she still had much to learn.

HOW TO START TELLING YOURSELF THE TRUTH

The difficulty of transitioning from a self-deceiving mode to a truth-telling mode depends in large part on the extent and duration of your self-deceptions. If you have been dishonest with yourself for a long time, it will be more difficult to find the truth and start being honest. Similarly, if you've been in denial about who you are at work (as opposed to what you do), you will have an even a steeper mountain to climb.

Luckily, it can be climbed! Leveling with yourself takes a certain amount of self-assessment, courage, and will, but you have complete control over the outcome. Accepting who you are starts by facing some hard truths you may have been fighting to hide, but everyone is capable of doing this. The ability to be okay with the admission of your flaws and shortcomings plays more of a vital role between you and yourself, not you and others. Remember, break-throughs start with breakdowns—breaking down your truths into digestible pieces.

To ensure you are being honest with yourself and being truthful with others, ask yourself the following questions:

- *What drives my behavior?*

Concentrate on some of the specific things you say or do at work, especially words spoken or actions taken that bother you in some way. Has your boss asked you to join him at a trade conference or departmental meeting? Did you tell him you would rather stay in the office and work on a project near deadline? Was that the real reason? Were you anxious about going? Were you trying to show your boss that you are your own person and won't do every-thing he suggests? Examine the underlying motivations to discover what's really going on inside of you. Don't be sat-isfied with easy or superficial answers. If you tell yourself, "I don't want to go to the trade show because those shows make me uncomfortable," ask yourself if you find your role at work uncomfortable; ask if your boss has anything to do with this discomfort. As the detectives say, "Get to the bottom of it." This is a rock that few people look under, yet those who do find powerful answers they didn't know existed, many of which create breakthrough possibilities in workplace performance.

• *What am I really passionate about?*

This is also a very telling question that can hit hard, but in a crucially necessary way. What gets you fired up, enthused, excited, and motivated to perform at your best? To get to the most revealing answer, ask yourself this question when you find yourself dissatisfied with what you are doing at work. Part of being honest with yourself means determining if your work is meaningful and fulfilling to you. Every job has parts that are a pain and that we'd prefer not to do or to delegate to others. But if you are not consistently passionate about what you are doing, whether you're a software designer or selling radio ads, you will not be able to hide from this truth very long. Dale Carnegie said, "You'll never achieve real success unless you like what you're doing."

• *Am I playing to win or not to fail?*

I was hired to coach Susan, the vice president of an architectural development firm, on her presentation skills. Her firm was vying to win business for a $550-million project and the partnering firm suggested that *everyone* get coached on their presentation skills, but I was sent in to target her behavior in front of a group, and I quickly learned why. When Susan got up to speak, she was robotic. She would stammer and look down and read the PowerPoint slides. How did the typical audience respond? They would lose confidence and interest both in her team and company. Why? She played not to fail. When I coached her alone, I told her to forget about the potential business. "In fact," I said, "stand up and tell me about your family members and all the things you love about them."

At first, Susan gave me a hesitant look, but I smiled supportively so up she stood, and a transformation ensued. When Susan talked about her spouse and three children, she beamed with energy and confidence. She not only emanated a magnetism of the type that builds relationships and gets results, but she proved she had teeth because she smiled!

This strategy works far and wide in all types of industries because it forces others to tell themselves that "playing not to fail" is more pervasive than they consciously realize. When high-level executives are serious and all business, it's usually fear-based behavior that detracts and turns away clients and employees instead of attracting them. What position are you playing from?

- *Am I apprehensive about being myself because I have to "act" a certain way?*

This is a complex but important distinction to make: be honest *with* yourself about whether you are truly *being* yourself. This is difficult because we do behave differently in different situations. How you interact with a client who is conservative and wants nothing but bottom-line data will differ from a direct report with whom you share a fervor for the same sports team that won a big game the night before. The ability to adapt is a critical component in your ability to develop results-producing relationships with a wide variety of people. However, while your behaviors may change, your authenticity and values should not.

A Defining Moment of Self-Realization

Many years ago, I was the opening keynote speaker for a sales convention with 1,900 attendees. It was a rowdy crowd and the energy and competitive spirit was through the roof. The connection I made with the group was good, the verbal feedback was good, and the written evaluations I read a week later were also good. But there are times when good stinks because you know you're capable of great or beyond. Then came the moment of truth.

A week later, the company who filmed the convention sent me a video copy of my keynote speech. Remember,

I coach presentation skills for a living, and as soon as I started watching the video, I intuitively knew something was missing. I meticulously critiqued my skills in the video. My gestures, eye contact, voice projection, movement, pausing, and body language were fluid and consistent. But still, something was missing. I watched the video for another 10 minutes, frustrated at my inability to see what it was, especially when I coach other people on it every day. Then it hit me like a linebacker drilling a quarterback on a blind-side blitz. Whammo!

I was not being myself. It's not that I wasn't sincere about my message or didn't believe every word I delivered. I was trying to be a great speaking professional instead of being myself, a person who possessed solid presentation skills. I put the performance before the authenticity, and it was the most refreshing slap in the face I'd taken in business up to that point. From that moment on, I realized, I would always **be myself first** and do my best to apply the skills required to build relationships and win business. The results have been astounding as I shed that insecurity: my confidence, connections, and results through relationships have headed straight north, and the stress of trying to be "the man" is all but gone. I couch this by admitting that my room for growth in business and relationships is boundless, but knowing that I'm operating from a core of self-truth is liberating beyond the workplace. But this would not have happened without the *third-person perspective* provided by the video, which leads to: *perception alignment*—a technique to uncover the absolute truth about you.

Perception Alignment

There is a major difference in how effectively most leaders/professionals *think* they connect with others versus how others *actually view* them, which is often worlds apart.

The obvious objective here is to bring those two dynamics closer together. We can do this by using a process called perception alignment. This process to close the gap between intent and perception begins with seeing what other people see in you to gain a third-person perspective. Moreover, this critical path toward great communication with others warrants an ego willing to accept brutal honesty for the purpose of growth.

As you know by now, feedback is an integral step in learning about who you are, earning the trust of others, improving your relationship skills, and developing an accurate assessment of your abilities. It is a terrific tool for building confidence, performance, and connections with others. In this context, it helps you determine if what you tell yourself internally is consistent with what the outside world perceives. To determine if a disconnect exists between who you think you are and how others perceive you, consider the following exercise:

- Contact four to seven reliable work colleagues who are familiar with your workplace performance and ask them if they would be willing to provide you with some honest feedback about your performance.

- Write a brief description of your strengths and weaknesses in the workplace; focus on what you feel you contribute to your organization and your team as well as where you might fall short.

- Send those who are willing to participate an assessment form with the following three questions:

    1. What should I start doing that would improve my performance in the workplace and my relationships with others?

    2. What should I stop doing that is hurting my performance and my relationships with others?

3. What should I continue doing that is helping my performance and enhancing my relationships with others?

- When you receive the responses, compare them with your own written description of strengths and weaknesses; identify the disconnects.

- If one (or more) of the people who provided you with feedback is willing, set up a meeting to discuss the disconnects and so that you can ask questions to help you understand the conflicting point of view; be open to what you hear.

Part of this process is similar to receiving a 360-degree assessment on your behavioral performance. However, the difference is that you are doing the legwork. The realistic downside is that some people will not be comfortable in engaging in the process. A very strong upside is that you will uncover insights and make breakthrough connections that impact your company's and your own bottom line, multifold.

In a three-year period with one client, my firm had 51 out of 52 executives from a major corporation say this process was one of the most powerful learning and growth experiences in their career. Many of these folks had been in business for 30+ years.

The perception alignment process works, but how you frame it up front is instrumental. Be sure to inform your participants that you're seeking transparently candid feedback for professional growth and development.

The following sample instructions may help you implement the process:

Dear Jane,

As I mentioned to you recently, I'm following up with an attached assessment of my leadership skills, performance, and behavior. (This will have the three questions mentioned previously.)

To help me reach a new level of improvement as a leader and contributor to our organization, *please make sure you are completely candid.* The only way for me to build on existing strengths and remove dangerous blind spots that may be hurting me, my team, or our organization is to know what these opportunities are.

Additionally, if you're willing, I'd like to set up a personal meeting to discuss your feedback for 20 to 30 minutes. Prior to our meeting, please e-mail me your responses so that I can look them over and prepare my questions. When we do meet, please provide three significant discussion points from your assessment:

1. Elaborate on my strengths, so that I may build on them for better performance.
2. Elaborate on my areas that most need improvement for better performance.
3. Offer suggestions or solutions that you believe may support my growth as a leader.

The dates I have available to discuss this are

1.
2.
3.

(Provide three options here that include 20-to-30 minute windows—again make sure they provide you with the completed assessment no later than 24 hours before your debriefing meeting).

I appreciate your honest and candid feedback. Thanks for your participation in making me a better leader.

Joe

One more suggestion: If the perception alignment process seems too bold for you to conduct alone, ask others to do it along with you. Have your team members swap questionnaires with each other or your sales team members swap questionnaires with customers. In all the years I've worked with professional organizations where participants committed to this exercise, increased knowledge and performance improvement behaviors were guaranteed.

Feedback Tools

More and more businesspeople are on autopilot and never question themselves or their abilities. They don't take time to analyze their concerns or fears with determination and honesty. Instead, they camouflage insecurities and deny that problems exist. Or they may just adopt an attitude— cynical and negative—that allows them to avoid asking or answering revealing questions.

Here are two useful ways you can uncover the truth about yourself and your abilities:

- *Use videotape of yourself to clarify the feedback.*

In other words, use visual evidence to determine if your outward communication (impact) is consistent with your internal voice (intent). Ideally, you will be able to find someone to videotape you in a variety of situations— presentations, meetings, one-on-one conversations, and so on. The less conscious you are of the camera, the more likely you are to act normally and create a useful tool to gauge and improve your skills. Generally, people forget about the camera after a while and revert to their natural styles. (And thinking that the camera puts on an extra 40 pounds isn't telling yourself the truth either.)

- *Practice talking honestly to yourself based on the feedback you've received and the questions you've asked yourself.*

You won't be talking to yourself out loud with strangers around as you walk to the train. Still, it may feel strange at first and may take practice to understand and accept the new reality you've discovered. Your reflex will be to revert to hiding behind old self-deceptions, especially in times of stress. When you make a mistake in a work situation, you may rationalize why it wasn't your fault, why it isn't indicative of a weakness or deficiency. Alternately, you may take a more negative view and magnify the mistake so much that it becomes more serious than it actually is. The only way to overcome these reflex responses is to keep asking yourself the questions noted earlier and keep soliciting feedback from reliable sources. These are the best ways to root yourself in reality and to reflect that reality in the truths you tell yourself. As you've experienced in heated situations, cooler heads prevail after things happen. The key to telling yourself the truth for stronger relationship performance is to tell yourself the truth as it's happening. This is easier written then executed, but application is key, and it all starts with disarming our biggest success stopper—the cynic within.

LEVELING WITH YOURSELF

The best thing about how we deal with ourselves, our ego, and our interpretation of the truth is that we are often granted the opportunity to turn things around. That was the case for Stephanie. She was a highly driven salesperson for a top Los Angeles radio station, and her confident, extroverted demeanor helped her achieve an impressive $300,000 annual income. Stephanie figured she had gone about as far as she could in radio sales and wanted more. A vast networker with many contacts, she left her company and took a job as business development manager for a successful commercial real estate firm. Her base salary was lower than it had been at the radio station, but her commission opportunities promised earnings of three or four times her radio income if she executed the projected sales plan. Though Stephanie didn't know a ton about commercial real estate, she had confidence in her people skills and an ability to connect with others.

The first year in her new job was challenging for Stephanie, both financially and emotionally. She didn't hit her quotas or drive as many new clients to the firm as she had promised. She also wasn't used to working in a traditionally male industry; the big-earning members of her particular firm were all men. During that first year, Stephanie told herself that the problem was sexism, that she wasn't a member of the "boys' club" and many potential clients were turning her down because she wasn't a man. Her ego prevented her from considering any other explanation as to why she was encountering problems.

Stephanie's boss, Derek, knew that the problems lay deeper, but he wanted Stephanie to discover them for herself. That's why after her annual review, he asked her to consider the following question: "What is your biggest obstacle to producing at the level both you and I know you're capable of?" He told her to take the weekend to reflect on that question and then have an answer for him on Monday.

On the drive home from work, Stephanie thought about the question and repeated what had become her litany: "I'm a woman in a male-dominated industry, and Derek can't see that because he's a man." Yet, the more she heard herself say that, the more she realized that her answer wasn't completely accurate. Certainly some prejudice existed, but it was more than that. At some point during the weekend, an epiphany hit Stephanie. Though it was tough for her to accept the revelation, she realized it was accurate.

"I am the biggest obstacle to my success," she told Derek when she met with him on Monday. "I've been letting the insecurities of being a woman and not knowing the industry say *no* to me before I gave anyone else a chance to say *yes*. But you didn't hire me to be the knowledge guru of commercial real estate, you hired me because I connect with people, network well, and generate interest and relationships even better."

Despite his confidence in Stephanie's abilities, Derek wasn't certain that she would be able to admit the truth about her fears to herself. That she had done so and was sincere about it reinforced his faith in her. More than that, he admired and respected Stephanie's willingness to recognize where she had gone wrong. He knew that was a difficult thing for someone like Stephanie—someone who had achieved a considerable amount of success in her career and whose self-confidence had been instrumental in achieving that success. Because of Stephanie's recognition of her truth, Derek became even more supportive of Stephanie than he had been in the past. He committed to spending more time educating her about the commercial real estate industry and helping her figure out a strategy that would result in more and better connections. Derek fulfilled this promise, and by Stephanie's second year with the firm, she had earned $875,000, and the firm's sales numbers increased by 22 percent.

Accepting shortcomings and overcoming obstacles erected by egos are not easy tasks. Facing these hard truths has a huge relationship payoff. As Stephanie learned, being honest with herself energized her boss to do more for her. In fact, even if Stephanie had simply faced her truth and acted on it (without telling Derek about it) the relationship would have benefited because Stephanie would have approached her job in a very different manner. The key, therefore, is leveling with yourself and asking others to do the same. Those who are constantly willing to look both inward and outward to seek the truth are those who improve business relationships and reap the rewards that come from those relationships.

CHAPTER NINE

Give More than People Expect

Want to learn something that is well within your control and that yields bottom-line business results?

Develop the consistent habit of giving more than you currently give.

Cynics and contrarians snap at this statement like a squirrel pinned in a corner and say, "If you're giving because you're told to, it doesn't work and it's manipulative."

Newsflash: Yes it does work! It's not manipulative; it's a brilliant behavioral strategy. Giving is making an investment in relationships just as physical fitness is an investment in your physical and mental well-being. Think about the times you don't feel like working out, but you exercise anyway. And how do you feel after your workout? Great!

Giving is an exercise. In romantic relationships and personal friendships as well in your business connections, we'd all be big liars if we didn't say there are times when we don't feel like giving or helping, but we do it anyway. And how do you feel after you give? Great!

My opening argument for this chapter is that you may have things backward. People *feel* a certain way and their behavior follows as if they don't have a choice. I challenge you to do the opposite. Commit to your behavior and earn the feeling of gratitude in your own investment simply because you did the right thing. Oh, and this behavioral strategy is almost a mathematical probability for making more money, expediting trust, and improving the workplace performance of those around you. Let's find out why.

Giving is a given in any business relationship. You are expected to give a certain amount of time and effort in any business relationship. If you are managing up, you give your boss what she needs to help her complete group tasks or meet objectives. If you are managing down, you give your direct report the information and support necessary for him to complete his assignments.

In the professional world, many people give only what is necessary rather than making an optimum investment, which can yield prolific, prodigious returns. They also give only what's requested or expected and limit both their contribution and perceived value. It's important to think beyond the scope of one's particular role. Creativity and courage may be the linchpin concepts that create break-throughs when it comes to giving.

The wonderful part of giving is that it need not be laborious in time or effort to garner significant outcomes. There are times when a kind word, a supportive idea, a short note, or serving as a sounding board can render reciprocal benefits for the giver. But it needs to be a priority on your radar, not a situational reflex or obligatory task.

By giving consistently and broadly, you will exceed your colleagues' expectations. And as you'll discover, when you give more than what is expected, you get more than you give. To help you understand this paradox, I will share with you a recent exchange of e-mails from a client.

GIVING IS AN ATTITUDE AS WELL AS AN ACTION

Mary, an employee of a midsize corporation, always gives her bosses more than they expect. On a recent assignment, she worked harder and more thoroughly than seemed possible. She gave not only her time but also her business acumen. This effort resulted in the following e-mail from Mary's boss to Mary as well as to other executives in the company:

> Team,
>
> I wanted to let you know about one of Mary's accomplishments this month. I just finished a thorough review of the January 2008 THL reporting package and have found that Mary completed the package with 100 percent accuracy. She came in on Sunday and finalized the package nearly from beginning to end, which included the 2008 new-year setup. Since Mary started last year on December 14th, this was her first investor reporting package new-year setup. She tied out each portfolio, as well as the top fund level, to the 2008 approved plan numbers and ensured that the prior year's numbers tied exactly to what was reported to the investors on December 31, 2007, at each statement line. Each schedule of this reporting package needed to be updated to present new-year information, which again, she did independently and 100 percent error free. This demonstrates her thorough understanding of the financial reporting product. Our customers are certainly scrambling and just as busy at this time of year, and she has finalized their information not only on time, but early, guaranteeing sufficient review time.
>
> Nice job Mary, your efforts on this report have really contributed to the team's goals at this aggressive time of year!!
>
> Very much appreciated.
>
> Sonya

Here is Mary's response to this e-mail:

Oh my goodness!
Thank you so much!!! I am completely speechless right now. . . . I love my team, and I truly enjoy what I do. I can't take all the credit for myself, I work with the best team members you can ever have, and it gives me a sense of fulfillment to be able to contribute to our success and productivity as a group. It was definitely my pleasure, thanks again.
Mary

By giving of herself fully, Mary received recognition for her efforts and contribution via an e-mail from her boss, which circulated upward to the CFO. That not only made her feel great, but also let key members of the executive team know that Mary had performed at an exceptional level. Mary's boss went out of her way to spread the news of Mary's accomplishments, and she did so because Mary provided her with a level of performance that went beyond the call of duty.

Mary has the type of giving attitude that makes everyone from customers to CEOs want to have her on their teams. Influential executives cannot do enough for people like Mary because they receive so much and naturally want to repay in kind.

Don't forget Sonya's contribution. Through her willingness to acknowledge the efforts of a job well done, do you think Mary's trust in the organization and performance will continue to improve? If more managers would provide recognition and motivate performance on a consistent basis, do you think it would influence the profitability of their companies?

Managers who believe "compensation is recognition enough" do not understand the value of influential leadership.

A giving attitude may not be something you have when you first start working, but as you read on you may discover new and additional ideas for making it a permanent fixture in all your business connections. Unfortunately, many of us don't go above and beyond to give our bosses, team members, or customers more than the minimum they expect. Why is that?

WHY WE FAIL TO GIVE AT THE OFFICE

Be honest with yourself: Is recognizing others in the workplace a consistent practice for you? In my years of corporate coaching, I've discovered that many people feel awkward or uncertain about doing more than what's expected for a boss or colleague. In fact, people fail to give to their fullest for the following five reasons:

1. *Insecurity.*

What would you say if you were asked to identify your CEO's best quality and communicate how much you appreciate that quality directly to him? What would be your first reaction at the prospect of having to do this? Would you feel anxious, intimidated, or disingenuous? At a loss for words? Worried that the CEO would think you had a hidden agenda—that you were angling for a promotion or pay raise?

These are all common responses. You don't want to take the risk of feeling uncomfortable. Your lack of comfort around this might also stem from feeling that such encouragement is inappropriate, that it's not your place to communicate such a sentiment to a person of influence in your workplace. (This is all assuming that you get along with and/or respect the person we're talking about here.) While you probably have less difficulty complimenting friends or family members, many clients express that doing so in a business setting seems unnatural and risky. It's easier to play it safe.

2. *Lack of disciplined habit.*

Everyone has workplace routines, and the odds are that giving encouragement, ideas, and more frequent assistance to your business partners isn't part of that routine. Instead, you have a series of standard practices designed to accomplish necessary tasks as well as habitual behaviors related to those tasks. These may include e-mailing bosses, colleagues, and clients to update them about your progress toward completing a project; having a cup of coffee with coworkers but not your boss; casual conversations with your customer about work-related matters but never about his career concerns.

This task-oriented thinking can limit what we can accomplish in business relationships; and as harsh as it may seem, do little to garner better results, faster. At this point, we may feel that if we vary from our routines, we'll be looked at strangely for breaking ranks. But as one of America's premier executive coaches, Marshall Goldsmith, aptly states, "What got you here won't get you there." Giving genuine recognition and encouragement needs to become a reliable habit when you invest in business relationships.

3. *Selfishness.*

To a certain extent, everyone places his or her own self-interest before others. But you don't have to let self-interest turn into selfishness. Nonetheless, in a world where people's jobs are getting downsized left and right and where politics plays a role in who gets ahead, people often become selfish and don't consider the other guy. The reason: If I don't benefit, why should he? People think it is wasted effort to help others achieve goals or to encourage them to pursue growth and development because they're not going to get anything out of it—or so it appears.

4. *No toolbox.*

Most people are never taught how to communicate positive encouragement to others. No one sat them down and said, "Here are your options for providing people of influence with support and ideas" or "Here are the ways you can really help someone in a position of authority." Lacking specific suggestions about how to go about giving, they don't do anything.

5. *Backward priorities.*

The task-oriented mentality of most business professionals often takes precedence over the execution of positive reinforcement, which is contradictory. If you compliment my behavior about how well I treat customers today, it's naturally going to motivate me to treat them even better tomorrow. Yet, people devote all their energies to getting a job done and don't invest the time or energy for anything else, even when those positive connections often don't take much time at all. They may recognize that giving, in various ways to relationship partners, is something they should do, but they just never get around to doing it. They don't grasp what most successful leaders understand: people always come before process.

These five reasons are significant obstacles that affect your ability to give above and beyond your relationship partners' expectations. To overcome these obstacles, it helps to identify them. When you recognize that your priorities are backward or that your selfishness and insecurity is preventing you from giving, your awareness helps you make a conscious effort to get beyond those barriers.

It also helps to have behavioral applications for making major contributions to those with whom you work or network. Sometimes, all it takes is knowing the various ways you can make a difference in your boss's or customer's professional life. With this in mind, let's examine your options for making an immediate impact.

MAKING CONTRIBUTIONS THAT COUNT

Do you know the old excuse that people offer about why they don't buy a gift for a spouse or a parent? It's something along the lines of, "There's nothing I can buy him because he has everything." People use the same faulty thinking at work. They assume that an executive has all he'll ever need of everything—advice, information, support, and ideas. In fact, most people, no matter how influential they might be, find these things in short supply.

Think about how you might make a contribution to a team member's success. While many others exist, there are four major categories of contributions:

1. *Contributing through education and mentoring upward*

   • Teach your boss or customer a technology-related skill that you are proficient in and that he or she is not.

   • Figure out where your relationship partner is information-deficient and find the information he needs.

   • Share lessons learned from your own experience that have to do with an issue that concerns your partner; give them the opportunity to talk, and *listen* to them.

   • Meet with customers/clients for knowledge exchanges free of charge; use these exchanges to communicate important trends and developments that may impact their businesses.

- Create a white paper, newsletter, or other communication tool that summarizes best practices in a given, relevant area.

2. *Contributing through candor**

- Challenge your boss or customer kindfidently with an idea (that you believe in) that contradicts the way she's always done things.

- Provide feedback about a recent presentation made by a member of your team with strengths and opportunities to improve.

- Point out potential danger spots in your client's business strategy.

- Be completely honest if you think your partner is hurting his career in some way.

3. *Contributing through opportunity and empowerment*

- Work on a new project on your own that has to do with a group goal or a professional objective of your partner; if you discover something of value, share what you've learned with him.

- Mentor someone in your group or in your customer's company who needs help breaking through to a new level when you know a colleague or boss would like to see them do well.

- Refer a vendor you trust and think highly of to your customer or client.

- Have your organization sponsor a charitable event that you know your client supports or one that focuses on an issue of personal concern to her.

---

*As mentioned in Chapter 3, the approach here needs to be prudent and diplomatic, but pushing back in the spirit of helping is what many professionals never received, particularly those holding executive positions.

4. *Contributing through recognition*

- Write a note or a memo that compliments your boss or customer on what you believe was a truly significant idea or other action; copy an influential person in your or their organization.

- Boost your relationship partner's morale when he's down; remind him of the skills and knowledge that make him effective and an attractive job candidate.

- When team members meet a tough deadline or submit a major proposal that is approved, take them out to dinner or do something to celebrate the accomplishment and the role they played; focus on having a great time.

- Practice positive talk directly to your team about the unique qualities and strengths of each individual; communicate how others' performance has helped your group achieve significant milestones.

HOW DO YOU KNOW WHAT TO CONTRIBUTE?

This question is one that perplexes people who want to go beyond the minimum expectations in business relationships but don't know how. They sincerely would like to help their boss achieve his career objectives or lend emotional support when he's down, but they don't know what those objectives are or when he's feeling down about work.

This is not an unusual situation. As mentioned in Chapter 6, we typically don't know nearly as much about the people for whom we work as we do about the people in our personal lives. While we may understand their work style preferences—perhaps they are sticklers for neatness—and they may give us the headlines about their lives—their child hit a home run to win his little league team's game—we are often ignorant about their hopes and dreams, anxieties and problems.

To remedy that situation, use the following *private investigator exercise*:

Make it your business to uncover essential truths about your relationship partner. Specifically, as part of your investigation, look for the following information:

- What part of his job is his biggest headache; what keeps him awake at night and causes him the most stress?
- What is her career dream; what does she hope to accomplish over the next 10 years?
- Is there something going on that is preventing him from performing at peak capacity, whether in his private or professional life?
- Is there someone in the organization that she has particular difficulty dealing with?
- What are the small things that make his day; does he like a specific type of coffee; is he in a better mood when someone helps him organize his office?
- What types of tasks does she hate to do—whether it's paperwork, going through e-mails, or sitting through meetings; what activities are especially aggravating?
- What does he feel is his biggest opportunity in the coming year to make an impact; what single project or responsibility is he most excited about?

To complete this exercise effectively, review the following tips:

- *Use rehearsed questions.* Think about the questions you want to ask to get the information you need to better meet the needs of your relationship partner. Plan when and what you're going to ask. For instance, think about how you might start a conversation to determine if your relationship partner is clashing with a colleague. Maybe you start by saying something like, "I heard Jim was put in charge of that new group; I wonder if he has the patience to deal with all those diverse people." This might evoke a better response than asking point blank, "Is it just me, or is Jim a hot-headed idiot?"

- *Catch the subtle reaction.* Observe your relationship partner closely. He may not be sufficiently open to respond verbally to all your questions, but if you observe his attitude and actions in various situations, you'll find answers to many of the questions. Grimaces and frowns and smiles and nods all give you a sense of how someone feels about a given individual or situation. Does your boss suddenly become animated when he talks about his weekend hobby? Does your customer become unusually quiet when his boss walks into the room? Paying close attention to the nuances of communication will give you a read on your relationship partner and areas where you can be helpful.

- *Pay attention to the chatter.* A good investigator recognizes that you can learn a lot about someone indirectly as well as directly. Obviously, a lot of office talk is nothing more than rumors and politics, and you need to separate the wheat from the chaff. Nonetheless, it is true what they say: everyone in an organization knows everyone else's business. Information about conflicts between people, ambitions, and idiosyncrasies are often accurate, and if you listen with a practiced ear, you'll learn about people of influence in your company (because people of influence are the ones people talk about most).

The impetus of this investigative work is not intrusive, gossipy, or prying. Instead, you need to know your boss, direct report, or customer better to know how to contribute better. You only possess so much time and energy, and this knowledge helps you focus your contributions in ways that are meaningful to your colleague. It's simply working smart versus only working hard. Let's look at some examples of specific types of contributions you can make.

CONTRIBUTION WORDS AND DEEDS

Anticipate Your Partner's Needs and Fill Them

It's almost as if you read her mind. Using questions, observation, and listening skills, you've figured out that your customer would love to know how a competitor's product that was introduced in China is doing. So you do the research and present it to her. She can't believe it. She tells you she was actually considering assigning you this job, but you somehow beat her to it.

Anticipating people's needs is a skill just about any diligent, observant person can acquire, and it is a skill that can truly cement relationships. Making this unexpected effort communicates not only that you care about what the other person wants but that you know her well enough to give it to her. This launches your credibility and enhances your reputation—which always follows you.

Communicate Quietly and Consistently That You're Paying Attention

You don't have to deliver the moon to contribute. You can surpass your partner's expectations in small ways as well as big ones. For instance, Kelly was an entry-level engineer at a Denver construction company. Her project team was in the process of building a $48 million building for a client, and they met with the client every Monday. Besides Kelly, the meeting was attended by the client, John, and his staff, as well as by members of Kelly's team, including a senior engineer, project manager, and operations manager, all of whom were senior to Kelly.

The meetings often became heated under the stress of trying to finish the project on time and under budget, resulting in raised voices and frequent arguments. Kelly was the only one who remained calm. She didn't speak much, but when she did, she would ask questions like, "John, what is the part of this project that concerns you the most?" or "What can we do to make sure you know we're providing the highest-quality work and service?"

Finally, after one too many unproductive arguments, John asked to meet with Kelly and no one else. Randy, the project manager, was insulted and sternly told John, "She's not in a position of authority."

"Randy," John said, "can you tell me what the single most important objective is for me to make this project successful?"

Randy stammered and took two guesses, both of which were wrong.

John explained that Kelly was sure of the answer and that she should be informed of changes in real time. He also explained that Kelly's ability to ask just the right questions and listen intently communicated that she was really paying attention and cared about John and the needs of his development team. As a result, he trusted her opinion, even though she lacked the experience and expertise of other members of the team. Ultimately, the project was completed on time and under budget, and Kelly's relationship with John helped her secure a promotion to senior engineer twice as fast as it would have normally taken.

Assume an Onerous Task

Everyone is busy in today's fast-paced world of constant change, yet you should be aware of times when a colleague may have tasks or responsibilities that are difficult for him, but easier for you. He may have difficulty documenting reports or contributing to an online newsletter. He may hate going to a particular conference or find a new piece of software difficult to master.

Now, of course, you need the skills and knowledge to do whatever you volunteer for; offering help in an area where you're unqualified to help will backfire. But if you're competent to do it, your efforts to help others when deadlines are looming and the pressure's on are great investments of team spirit that frequently show up later in positive returns.

Ask for Nothing

This is what I refer to as the *need-nothing* tool. It consists of reaching out to a direct report or colleague and not making a request for anything. You simply touch base with them to see how they are doing or if you can assist them with anything. Most people don't realize how consistently they ask for something when they meet with their business colleagues. They always have an agenda—hidden or otherwise—that is the real purpose of the meeting.

By asking for nothing, you give yourself the chance to contribute, which isn't always possible when you want something. Even though it might seem otherwise, your relationship partner is probably aware from the moment you start talking whether you are planning to ask for something. People quickly detect I-want-something signals. By freeing yourself from the confines of a beggar role, you open up fresh possibilities for the relationship. You communicate that you are there to listen, offer ideas, and provide support—that this time the conversation is about him, not you. In turn, this attitude encourages your relationship partner to open up. For the first time in the relationship, he might be willing to share a deeper fear or concern with you. At the very least, he may ask you for suggestions or ideas on a topic of concern to him rather than spending all the time trying to help you with your challenges.

GIVE FROM THE HEART AS WELL AS FROM THE HEAD

Every day, you have tasks that must be completed, and it's easy to get so caught up in your own schedule that making the effort to help others gets placed on the very back burner. Few of these action items happen with consistency and that's why I have clients either schedule them or capture them in writing so that they have the tools to apply in front of them.

You may have the best intentions, but contributing to other people's success in business isn't something that is naturally at the top of your priority list. Write yourself a note promising that this week, you're going to stop by your boss' office and ask either how you can help or what you can do better to make his life easier. Scheduling offers an informal commitment that you will follow through on your best intentions.

Finally, keep in mind that the best way to contribute to others is not always the most obvious one. For instance, lifting a customer's spirits when her company is going through turmoil may be a far greater contribution than providing her with a discount on her next order. Read people, study them, and listen to them. Be a student of human interaction, and you will ratchet up your own perceptiveness and develop an uncanny intuition about how to help others and the best time in which to do so.

Again, little openings create big opportunities for contribution. If you're talking to your vendor on the phone, and you can tell he seems edgy, don't just blow it off; ask the question, "Terry, is everything okay? You don't seem yourself." That very question may allow him to say, "Sorry, it's just that our company is in the process of a buyout, and no one feels very secure around here right now." Lending an ear seems like a natural reaction of support. But go the extra step and later that day or the following day, leave a voicemail or drop an e-mail saying, "Terry, was thinking about our phone call earlier. Sorry you're going through a challenging time. Try to keep your spirits up and hang in there."

As I've learned from my own experiences in reaching out to others who have shown this type of support, it is often this going "beyond the transaction" that later results in transactions. So many businesspeople think emotional support has no impact on the bottom line; however, being able to offer emotional support is a character trait that breeds trust, loyalty, and long-term business.

CHAPTER TEN

Maximize Your Return on Relationships

While I've had the privilege to speak to and coach clients in a wide variety of industries, you've probably surmised that I've worked quite a bit with construction professionals. Many of them are big, hearty, tough guys. They're smart and rugged, but there's one question I've asked that has rocked even the toughest managers: "When your career is over, what kind of leader do you want to be remembered as?"

This is a question that I started asking at the conclusion of more intimate leadership and executive development programs. The responses to this simple inquiry have provided insights and intelligence beyond what I'd ever imagined.

First, not a single program participant has ever said: "I want to be known as a leader who made a million dollars before the age of 40" or "I hope I'm remembered as a smart executive who shredded the dignity of others to get the job done."

What people answer with has profoundly impacted the awareness of their peers and even themselves in the very moment they stand and deliver it in front of a group.

Some of the answers have included: "When my career is over, I hope I'm known as an individual who put his team before his own interests." or "I want to be known as a guy who greeted people like they mattered." or "As a leader who gave others a chance to succeed in their careers because so many others gave me a chance."

Are you noticing a theme here? Almost every single participant, to a person, discusses their relationships with others before the business process. The tragic irony, however, is that what many professionals say and do are in utter opposition. They put the process before the person. They put themselves before the team. They put the dollar before the relationship.

On some level, this is easy to understand. It's business, right? Strategy, mission, vision, and bottom-line results need to be achieved. Perform or you're out. It's a dog-eat-dog world. I understand, having run my own business for many years, yielding a profit is required to stay afloat.

However, let me offer another bottom-line statement: If your company is a race car and the track it speeds around is the business world, then the engine inside your car represents your relationships. You may be the driver of the car but if you're on autopilot, you're in trouble. You need to fine-tune that engine, understand the value it brings to your car, and make sure you are maintaining and improving performance at all times.

So, as we make our final turn (yes, I risk vulnerability and corniness in my feeble attempt at humor), I want to leave you with something that will both inspire you to strive for results-producing relationships and facilitate the process as you go forward. The inspiration is necessary because it is easy to forget what you've learned here and not apply it to your life. Under the stress of deadlines or because of the complacency of achievement, you may neglect your key relationships and reverse what needs to be a priority at all times.

At the same time, even if you are motivated to form these powerful partnerships, you may encounter some obstacles along the way. Maybe there's a boss who doesn't want to reciprocate your own actions of listening, recognizing, and being completely honest. Perhaps you find yourself unable to be as honest with yourself as a partnering relationship requires. Some going-forward advice may help clear up these and a plethora of other obstacles.

I also will address the common questions and doubts that might occur to you as you become committed to a relationship partnering path—questions and doubts that often arise when people attempt to move key relationships to a higher level.

Let's start out with a chart that makes a convincing argument for investing continuously in your business relationships.

REMIND YOURSELF WHY YOU PARTNER

Over the years, I've worked with many powerful and influential leaders, and though their personalities were all different, the ones who had the highest accomplishments of success shared one skill: relationship building. In fact, it's not just the leadership layer of organizations that demonstrate this ability but just about everyone who is tabbed a high potential as well as the most successful entrepreneurs. All of them have at least a few key partnering relationships, ones where self-honesty, productive confrontation, open communication, and the like keep those relationships ongoing and strong.

Some people will tell you that if you want to succeed now and in the future, you need to master technology skills. Others insist that the key to getting ahead is making astute decisions about the jobs you take (and the ones you turn down). Still others believe that being a great networker is key.

While networking is the closest traditional model of the career advice I'm suggesting, most networking boils down to working a room and collecting business cards. Or it involves initiating conversations and communicating often with a lot of different people.

There is nothing wrong with any of that, but if you don't dig deep, you greatly diminish your changes of cultivating the type of relationships that can elevate your position, recognition, and success at work. Networking is making a series of small, simple investments in relationships. I'm asking you to make more significant and deeper investments. If you do, you can expect major returns, as detailed in Table 10.1.

This is only a sampling of the types of investments made and returns received. Throughout the book, I've described other types of investments and returns. Still, this chart provides a good motivational shorthand, one you can refer to with team members when strategizing about how to boost client results or when you're wondering about making the effort that partnering relationships demand.

Consider that it's not only you who benefit from your higher-level relationships but team members, other departments, and your organization at large. Though I've focused on individual career and effectiveness benefits, I can guarantee you that organizations with strong relationships among employees also have strong bottom-line results. When a critical mass of individuals are partnering with their colleagues, organizations reap the following benefits:

- Higher employee trust and loyalty
- Stronger morale and motivation
- Aligned understanding of company vision and mission
- Better recruiting and retention results
- Increased ability to attract new customers/clients
- Faster development of leaders with strong people skills

Table 10.1 Investments and Returns on Relationships

Relationship Investments		Positive Returns
Higher self-awareness, willingness to show vulnerability and admit fault	*Results in*	Increased respect from boss and clients
Viewing self as a partner	*Results in*	Higher self-confidence Respected reputation with colleagues and customers Smarter, assertive decisions
Great listening skills	*Results in*	Better understanding of how to meet others' needs Strong interviewing skills and talent management
Recognizing others	*Results in*	Improved morale, loyalty, and performance of team members
Productive confrontations	*Results in*	Trust of client, peers, and boss who count on you for reliable, candid feedback
Telling yourself the truth	*Results in*	Promotions due to honest self-assessments and continual improvement

Increasing the presence of partnering in your workplace will also help eliminate a great deal of suspicion, personality conflicts, and other negatives that plague many organizations, and finally, partnering fosters communication and empathy that crosses traditional boundaries (between different hierarchical levels or between customer and supplier).

I trust that all of this provides you with the ongoing motivation to establish and maintain results-producing relationships. But if this is not enough, let me supply another reason that you may not have considered.

A RELATIONSHIP-DRIVEN WORLD

Partnering relationships have always been important, but they are especially critical today. The right relationships with a boss or customer can make the difference between being employed or staying in business; it can make the difference between doing pretty well and doing outstanding. Social, economic, business, and technological trends are all elevating the importance of trusting and honest relationships. To understand how this is so, consider these key trends and how they've impacted relationships.

Technology

We live in a virtual world, more so now than ever before. We communicate with each other online rather than face-to-face or even phone-to-phone. Because of the technological wizardry being introduced and embraced by the workplace, we're going to become more virtual in the future. Yet at the same time, businesspeople are tired of technological interactions. They're bored by PowerPoint and overwhelmed by e-mail.

So while technology has made it possible to conduct business without seeing the other person, a backlash against this technology has emerged. It shouldn't be surprising that people are increasingly reluctant to do deals or brainstorm or discuss important issues without a face-to-face meeting. More to the point, if they are going to communicate virtually with people on key matters, they want to establish real relationships with them first. This means that individuals who can create true partnering relationships fast stand the best chance of being promoted or getting the business. They're the ones people will trust in an electronic world where trust is hard to come by.

Over the last five years, I'd need a hundred hands to count how many employees are disgruntled with the rudeness of bosses distracting meetings by checking their handheld electronic devices. This sense of entitlement is killing morale, violating trust, and insidiously poisoning organizational performance.

Don't get me wrong, I think e-mail, cell phones, and BlackBerries are amazing inventions. But where's the instruction manual on how to use them respectfully and professionally?

There is a growing need for strong relationships because of the dehumanizing nature of this technology. In fact, here's a mantra that communicates just that:

Relationships, not technology, build trust.
Relationships, not technology, improve performance.
Relationships, not technology, increase profit.

Global and Diverse Populations

If we are going to work successfully with people who are unlike ourselves in terms of background, belief, and traditions, then forming strong partnering relationships is crucial. In the past, we could collaborate with suppliers, customers, and colleagues based on shared norms. We came from similar educational systems, went through the same type of training, and emerged with a common way of working.

Now, the most important person in our world of work may be on the other side of the globe. If you don't know how to forge transparent, empathetic relationships, you are

likely to struggle when you try to work with someone who
has very different work habits from you. Just as important, the global nature of work means that you no longer
have as much face-to-face time with your boss, customers,
or direct reports. Technology is a poor substitute for one-
on-one conversations. What is a good substitute, however,
is creating and maintaining a relationship where trust is
absolute and openness and honesty are givens. When
you have the opportunity, you must strike with a positive,
reciprocally benefiting impact.

Rapid and Far-Reaching Change

Strong, stable relationships are anchors during volatile
times. The nature of your job and your organization may
change radically, but if you partner with people, you always
have someone to turn to and rely on—and vice versa.
Mergers, acquisitions, downsizing, restructuring, high turn-
over, job changes, and so on can all leave you feeling uncertain and insecure. During these times, you need someone
to turn to for advice, to provide you with support and
resources, and to lend a sympathetic ear.

People who are only superficial networkers are going to
struggle during times of change. They may know everyone,
but they don't know anyone that well. As a result, they are
essentially going to be on their own as their organizations
go through upheavals. Not only might they find their jobs
in jeopardy because they don't enjoy a partnering relationship with their bosses, but they may also feel isolated and
alone.

Alternatively, if you make a consistent effort to establish relationship partnerships, you're going to survive and
thrive no matter what happens. If you lose your job, you
have people out there that will bend over backward to help
you find another one. If you lose one customer, another
customer will step forward and provide you with a lead

to an even better one. If you reach a career crossroads because of all the changes in your company or industry, you have someone you trust and respect who will help you sort through the complexities of what to do next.

TROUBLESHOOTING: HOW TO KEEP PARTNERING RELATIONSHIPS IN GOOD SHAPE

Expect some bumps along the way. When you're dealing with people, anything can happen. If you're a veteran professional, you know that there's still a lot you don't know and can't know until you go through it.

Someone thinks he has a good relationship with a boss and a week later he's out of a job. You may believe you and your client are of one mind, and then it becomes clear you have major philosophical differences. In short, you've followed this book's advice, but things didn't work out as you expected.

Don't get thrown by relationship snafus. They happen. In fact, they happen in all caring, compassionate relationships. When you're honest and vulnerable with each other, you may say or hear something that creates problems.

The good news is these problems usually can be solved. The key is being alert for them and knowing what to do when they arise. To that end, here is a troubleshooting guide—in the form of questions and answers—that will help you deal with some common business relationship issues:

Question: I thought I was doing a great job establishing an open, honest relationship with my boss, and we've reached a point of being kind of open and kind of vulnerable, but can't get beyond that level. What should I do?

Answer: First, be honest with yourself about your own behavior. Are you pushing your boss too hard too fast? Some people need more time and experience working with someone before they open up or extend their trust. Second, consider what your boss really needs from the relationship and whether you're providing it. Perhaps he needs you to be a better listener. Maybe he would benefit if he could talk to you about his career frustrations. Once you find out what it is he really needs, then it's likely you can progress the relationship beyond the point where you're currently stuck.

Question: As hard as I try, I can't get people in my organization to respond to me in the way you say relationship partners should respond. Maybe it's the culture of our organization, but people seem reluctant to reveal their fears or engage in productive confrontation. Is there anything I can do to change this?

Answer: Even if your culture is highly politicized and discourages open communication, you should be able to find someone who is receptive to partnering. If you find your boss is resistant, try your boss's boss or someone of influence in another group or division. Or focus on customers and clients. Don't limit yourself to one or two possibilities. If your company employs 1,000 people, the odds are good that more than a few of them value deep, mutually empowering business relationships. Lateral management and external relationships are just as vital as those that run up and down.

Question: Partnering with people in my own organization is fine, but I'm finding it harder to establish this type of empathetic and open relationship with my customers. Should I change the process with "outsiders"?

Answer: The process should be equally effective with everyone, no matter where they work. That stated, the more you study and observe people, the more accurate you will be in your navigation. It may take a bit longer to establish a partnering relationship with a customer, in large part because you may not see him as often as you see someone who works right down the hall. This means you need to make a greater effort to communicate with this individual—arrange more lunches, try to meet more regularly, get together when you're at the same trade shows. Consistent human contact is essential for any relationship partnership.

Question: I have a great relationship with my mentor who is a senior executive in my organization, and he's done a lot to help my career. But the relationship still reflects our respective positions in the organization. He is always dispensing advice, and I'm always listening; he is the one who always complains, and I'm the one who offers a sympathetic ear. How can I change things so our relationship roles are more equal?

Answer: Level with your relationship partner. Express your gratitude for how he's helped your career, but communicate clearly that you feel the relationship is one-sided in certain ways and you want to work with him to change it to a true partnership. Employ a prefacing question like, "Bob, can I be completely honest with you?" It's likely that he's unaware that you feel this way, and if you communicate it to him with sincerity and without recrimination, he'll rethink how he relates to you.

Question: I've partnered with a member of my organization, but even though we're following the steps you suggest, the relationship isn't yielding results. We're engaging in productive confrontation, we're listening to each other better, but our work product remains the same. What are we doing wrong?

Answer: You can try a few things. First, you might just need to give the relationship more time to produce results. Relationships develop their power incrementally—it's an evolving process of learning to be more trusting, communicative, and supportive. You may not see results for weeks or even months. Be patient. Second, look for new or challenging projects to work on. Sometimes, it takes a stretch assignment to bring out the full capacity of a partner relationship. Third, ask for help from your partner, and encourage him to call on you for assistance. You need to be honest with each other about what you require, and your request can catalyze action, which is what produces positive outcomes. Own the behavior that will lead you in this direction.

Question: I feel awkward and ineffectual when I try to do the things you suggest. I wonder if I'm confronting productively or if I'm just engaging in counterproductive arguments. I've attempted to reveal my flaws without fear, but I suspect I'm not doing a good job of communicating what those fears are. Is there any way I can improve how I do these things?

Answer: Obtain feedback. This is the single best tactic for improving your relationship partnering skills. Certainly you should ask your partner for his opinion about how you're doing using these skills, but also get feedback from other people with whom you work closely. Are you doing a good job of listening deeply? Have you overcome your reluctance to confront? Constructive feedback obtained continuously will help you improve your partnering skills.

Question: I think I enjoy good partnering relationships with my boss and a client, but I'm intimidated when I attempt to establish this type of relationship with one of our company's top people. I'm convinced they'll think I'm being too pushy or trying to deal with them as equals while they're clearly way above me in the corporate hierarchy. So what can I do to overcome this intimidating feeling?

Answer: The biggest heckler is the cynic within, so start with positive self-talk. I've coached many senior vice presidents who need to practice this in communication with their company presidents. Few are immune from this upward relationship challenge. You need to find out more about their core values, needs, fears, and interests in and out of the workplace. It may be something that seems inane like the fact that in the eight years you've worked together, you never knew that you both had grandfathers who served in World War II. Seeking those connections as a habit almost always leads to common ground. Common ground is an entry point and the fuel for developing a partnering relationship. On the business level, it may serve you well to voice a straight question like, "What advice would you give me to bring my performance to a new level in the next six to twelve months?" You'd be shocked by how few people never ask this question.

DON'T PLACE LIMITS ON YOUR BUSINESS RELATIONSHIPS

The more relationships you can establish like the ones I've described, the more results you'll produce. It's a numbers game, one that can increase the numbers in your bank account if money is a core motivation for you.

While the logical first relationship partner is your boss or your customer, you can build these relationships with just about any type of work colleague. You may form strong bonds with two or three people with whom you work at a client company. You may establish close relationships not only with your boss but also with a key direct report and someone who is a member of your team. You may have a mentor with whom you establish a more equal relationship or a supplier with whom you work frequently.

Realistically, you only have so much time and energy for your relationships, and while it would be great if you could partner with the gal from the mailroom as well as your CEO, that's not always possible. You don't work closely with the mail gal, and if you're in a large organization and aren't yet in management ranks, you may also not have many (or any) encounters with the CEO. Other people, too, may lack the time, energy, or inclination to form relationships for results.

Keep your mind open about all of the relationship possibilities before you. Don't rule someone out because they're too high up in the organization . . . or too low. Managers find that establishing partnering relationships with their direct reports greatly increases their group's productivity—meetings run much more smoothly and effi-ciently when everyone is willing to confront and also will-ing to listen. No one is embarrassed about suggesting risky, innovative ideas or asking silly questions. People are up front about their fears and concerns, avoiding the behaviors that result when people have hidden agendas.

Be aware, too, that you may be able to form partnering relationships with people who seem obstinate, aggressive, reserved, or otherwise difficult. It's astonishing how quick we are to judge our work colleagues and label them. Many times, we haven't taken the time or made to effort to get to know them and get past their surface idiosyncrasies. This is especially true when you're dealing with someone of influ-ence who is highly demanding, critical, or hot tempered. In short, they're intimidating, and you can't imagine them being willing to listen deeply to what you have to say let alone being empathetic. Yet people can surprise you when you work hard at getting to know them and letting them get to know you. Once you get past a boss's gruff exterior, you might find someone who (consciously or not) has been look-ing for someone at work he can confide in and who is willing to challenge him when he says something that isn't right.

RECIPROCITY: THE IMPORTANCE OF
SCRATCHING BACKS

I've emphasized what you need to do to create partnering work relationships, but the effort must be reciprocated. You may do everything right from a partnering standpoint but still fail to create a relationship that creates results. That's because the other person refuses to reciprocate. Or he reciprocates infrequently or only in certain ways—in exchange for your listening, empathy, innovative ideas, and productive confrontation, your boss gives you regular raises and good bonuses. This is an unequal exchange.

Obviously, there's not much you can do if someone refuses to reciprocate. It's important, though, to keep the ideal of reciprocity in mind as you move forward in a relationship. Remember that reciprocity represents a fair, rather than perfectly equal, exchange. On one hand, your boss can give you things because he's a boss that you can't give him; your customer can offer assistance that you may not be able to offer in return. On the other hand, you can offer them other things that they may not be able to provide. You may be terrific at providing emotional support when they're going through crises, while they are great at finding you additional resources to accomplish tasks. This is reciprocity, even though it doesn't represent an exchange of the exact same thing.

To help you fix a reciprocity ideal in your head, let me tell you a bit more about Michael Viollt, who became president of Robert Morris College in 1995 and whose astonishing accomplishments include a 300 percent enrollment increase, the addition of five campuses and a graduate school, and developing an intercollegiate athletic program with 34 sports teams. Though Michael is a terrific, visionary leader, he didn't accomplish all these things alone. Instead, he relied on reciprocal relationships with other people.

Two of those people are Mablene Krueger and Nancy Rotunno. Mablene started as a teacher at Robert Morris in 1980, and over the last year, became the college provost. Over the years, she's worked closely with Michael and helped him launch and implement his vision; and in return, she's received great responsibility, but also more direct partnering benefits. As she says, "Mike showed trust in me from the very beginning and has been transparent about sharing important information, making it easy to trust his vision and leadership."

Nancy joined the school in 1982 as a counselor and is now the executive director for the college's Culinary Institute. The Institute has been a key part of Michael's growth strategy for the college, and Nancy has worked with him on executing that strategy, providing him with great commitment and energy. In turn, she says of Mike, "He has always been constructively critical and allowed mistakes. His faith in me instantly built my self-confidence and removed barriers to achievement."

Mike himself points to reciprocity as the key to the results-producing relationships he enjoys with Mablene, Nancy, and other members of his staff. He uses the term, "educated loyalty," to refer to his belief that people should not follow leaders blindly but grasp the vision for the organization and be willing to work to realize it based on that understanding.

"What's made our relationship so reciprocal is the execution of loyalty, each of us standing by the other even in times of adversity. This breeds total commitment." This is a solid definition of reciprocity and one that you can use an ideal for your own relationships.

THERE'S ONLY SO MUCH ONE MAN (OR WOMAN) CAN DO, BUT NO LIMIT TO WHAT TWO CAN ACCOMPLISH

What do you want your legacy to be? What do you hope to accomplish in your career?

No matter how you answer those two questions, building better relationships must be a large part of the answer.

Too often, we think of our work goals in the first person singular: "This is what I want to do; this is my goal." In reality, you can't get much done by yourself. Years from now, when you look back at your career and job achievements, you'll see how different relationships played critical roles in your achievements. Your success is tied to how successful you are at forming partnering relationships.

If you don't want to take it on faith, think about a particular achievement in your own career. Perhaps you received a promotion. Perhaps you completed a stretch assignment successfully. Whatever job task or career milestone you decide on, ask yourself the following questions:

- Could I have achieved what I did without assistance from another individual?
- Along the way, did someone provide a key piece of information or a good idea that helped me achieve my goal?
- Did I receive emotional support that helped me make it through a challenging period?
- Would I have had the opportunity for this achievement if someone hadn't stood up for me and insisted that I could handle the job?
- Did I team with one or more people to achieve the objective; did they provide the knowledge and skills that I lacked?

If you have only typical business relationships—mostly casual associations that focus on getting tasks done—then you'll reap some benefits. But if you value and nurture your business relationships in the ways I've described in this book, you'll enjoy a serious competitive advantage throughout your career. You'll find that people will have your back when you make a mistake. You'll discover that customers want to do business with you and executives want you on their teams. People will refer business to you. You will get the promotions you want and the jobs you've been dreaming about.

In other words, your relationships will produce great results.

But not just for you. Partnering relationships are mutually beneficial, and so you not only derive satisfaction and meaning from your own accomplishments but also from those of your relationship partners. During the course of your career, you'll help the people you care about obtain their dream jobs and make decisions about everything from transferring to retirement. You'll be there for them just as they're there for you.

We hear all this talk that there's no loyalty in business today. Employee dissatisfaction and customer complaints climb. There's no camaraderie. The fun has gone out of work. Unfortunately, many of these claims are indeed factual and statistically supported. But I will continue to wave the flag of support about people, for people, and with people. I've been given a special gift to be able to work with incredibly smart, successful businesspeople who know that no matter what position they hold or what business they are in, they will always be in the relationship business first. I hope you feel the same way and take the action steps necessary to produce the wonderful results that relationships bring.

When we seek to discover the best in others, we somehow bring out the best in ourselves.

—William Arthur Ward

INDEX